SPECTRUM
Test Practice

Grade 6

Published by Spectrum
an imprint of
Frank Schaffer Publications®

SPECTRUM

Editors: Alyson Kieda and Jeanine Manfro

Frank Schaffer Publications®

Spectrum is an imprint of Frank Schaffer Publications.

Send all inquiries to:
Frank Schaffer Publications
3195 Wilson Drive NW
Grand Rapids, Michigan 49544

Spectrum Test Practice—grade 6

ISBN: 1-57768-976-3

3 4 5 6 7 8 9 10 PHXBK 09 08 07 06 05 04

Introduction 6
Letter to Parent/Guardian 7
Correlation to Standards.................................8

Reading
Vocabulary
Synonyms 11
Vocabulary Skills.................................12
Antonyms 13
Multi-Meaning Words 14
Words in Context....................................15
Word Study 16
Sample Test: Vocabulary.........................17

Comprehension
Main Idea 21
Recalling Details 22
Inferencing/Drawing Conclusions.....................23
Fact & Opinion/Cause & Effect 25
Story Elements 26
Fiction 27
Nonfiction 32
Sample Test: Reading Comprehension..........37
Reading Practice Test: Answer Sheet............41
Reading Practice Test 42

Language
Mechanics
Punctuation 56
Capitalization and Punctuation 58
Sample Test: Language Mechanics 61

Language Expression
Usage..65
Sentences 68
Paragraphs..71
Sample Test: Language Expression................75
Spelling 79

Sample Test: Spelling...............................81
Study Skills 83
Sample Test: Study Skills...........................85
Language Practice Test: Answer Sheet 88
Language Practice Test.........................89

Math
Concepts
Numeration...100
Number Concepts 102
Properties..104
Fractions and Decimals 106
Sample Test: Concepts 108

Computation
Operations with Whole Numbers 110
Operations with Fractions 111
Operations with Decimals 114
Sample Test: Computation 117

Applications
Geometry 119
Measurement 122
Problem Solving....................................124
Algebra...128
Sample Test: Applications 129
Math Practice Test: Answer Sheet 133
Math Practice Test.................................134

Science and Social Studies
Science
Science 142
Sample Test: Science................................146
Science Practice Test: Answer Sheet 147
Science Practice Test...............................148
Social Studies
Social Studies 149
Sample Test: Social Studies.......................152
Social Studies Practice Test: Answer Sheet 153
Social Studies Practice Test........................154
Answer Key 155

With increased accountability in ensuring academic success for all learners, testing now takes a significant amount of time for students in all settings. Standardized tests are designed to measure what students know. These tests are nationally normed. State tests are usually tied to specific academic standards identified for mastery.

For many students, testing can be a mystery. They fear not doing well and not knowing what to expect on the test. This *Spectrum Test Practice* book was developed to introduce students to both the format and the content they will encounter on tests. It was developed on the assumption that students have received prior instruction on the skills included. This book is designed to cover the content on a representative sample of state standards. The sampling of standards is found on pages 8–10 with a correlation to the skills covered in this book and a correlation to sample standardized tests. Spaces are provided to record the correlation to the tests being administered by the user of this book. Spaces are also provided to add standards that are specific to the user.

Features of *Spectrum Test Practice*

- Skill lessons, sample tests for subtopics, and comprehensive content area tests
- Clues for being successful with specific skills
- Correlation of skills to state standards and standardized tests
- Format and structure similar to other formal tests
- Written response required in the Science and Social Studies sections
- Reproducible for use by a teacher for a classroom

Overview

This book is developed within content areas (Reading, Language, Math, Science, and Social Studies). A comprehensive practice test follows at the end of the content area, with an answer sheet for students to record responses. Within each content area, specific subtopics have been identified. Sample tests are provided for each subtopic. Within each subtopic, specific skill lessons are presented. These specific skill lessons include an example and a clue for being successful with the skill.

Comprehensive Practice Test

A comprehensive practice test is provided for each content area. The subtopics for each area are identified below:

- **Reading**
  - Vocabulary (synonyms, antonyms, multi-meaning words, words in context, foreign words, root words, and affixes)
  - Reading Comprehension (main idea, recalling details, sequencing, inferencing, drawing conclusions, fact and opinion, cause and effect, authors purpose, and story elements in fiction and nonfiction articles)
- **Language**
  - Language Mechanics (capitalization and punctuation)
  - Language Expression (usage, sentences, and paragraphs)
  - Spelling (both correct and incorrect spelling)
  - Study Skills (dictionary skills, reference materials, card catalog, reading tables and graphs, book parts)

- **Math**
  - Concepts (numeration, number concepts, fractions and decimals, and properties)
  - Computation (operations with whole numbers, fractions, and decimals)
  - Applications (algebra, geometry, measurement, and problem solving)
- **Science***
  - Plant/Animal Classification
  - Forms of Matter
  - Makeup of the Earth
  - Human Body
  - Astronomy
- **Social Studies***
  - The Americas
  - Europe
  - Ancient Civilizations
  - Map Skills
  - Economics

*Since states and often districts determine units of study within Science and Social Studies, the content in this book may not be aligned with the content offered in all courses of study. The content within each area is grade level appropriate. It is based on a sampling of state standards. The tests in Science and Social Studies include both multiple choice and written answer.

Comprehensive Practice Test Includes

- Content Area (i.e. Language)
- Subtopics (i.e. Language Mechanics)
- Directions, examples, and test questions
- Separate answer sheet with "bubbles" to be filled in for answers

Sample Tests

Sample tests are included for all subtopics. These sample tests are designed to apply the knowledge and experience from the skill lessons in a more formal format. No clues are included. These sample tests are shorter than the comprehensive tests and longer than the skill lessons. The skills on the test items are presented in the same order as introduced in the book.

Sample Tests Include

- Subtopic (i.e. Language Mechanics)
- Directions, examples, and test questions

Skill Lessons

Skill lessons include sample questions and clues for mastering the skill. The questions are formatted as they generally appear in tests, whether the tests are standardized and nationally normed or state specific.

Skill Lessons Include

- Subtopic (i.e. Language Mechanics)
- Skill (i.e. Punctuation)
- Directions and examples
- Clues for completing the activity
- Practice questions

Use

This book can be used in a variety of ways, depending on the needs of the students. Some examples follow:

- Review the skills correlation on pages 8–10. Record the skills tested in your state and/or district on the blanks provided.
- Administer the comprehensive practice test for each content area. Have students use the sample answer sheet in order to simulate the actual testing experience. The tests for Reading, Language, and Math are multiple choice. Evaluate the results.

- Administer the sample test for the subtopics within the content area. Evaluate the results.

- Administer the specific skill lessons for those students needing additional practice with content. Evaluate the results.

- Use the skill lessons as independent work in centers, for homework, or as seatwork.

- Prepare an overhead transparency of skill lessons to be presented to a group of students. Use the transparency to model the skill and provide guided practice.

- Send home the Letter to Parent/Guardian found on page 7.

Clues for Getting Started

- Determine the structure for implementing *Spectrum Test Practice*. These questions may help guide you:

  - Do you want to assess the overall performance of your class in each academic area? If so, reproduce the test practice and sample answer sheet for each area. Use the results to determine subtopics that need additional instruction and/or practice.

  - Do you already have information about the overall achievement of your students within each academic area? Do you need more information about their achievement within subtopics, such as Vocabulary within Reading? If so, reproduce the sample tests for the subtopics.

  - Do your students need additional practice with some of the specific skills that they will encounter on the standardized test? Do you need to know which students have mastered which skills? These skill lessons provide opportunities for instruction and practice.

- Go over the purpose of tests with your students. Describe the tests and the testing situation, explaining that the tests are often timed, that answers are recorded on a separate answer sheet, and that the questions cover material they have studied.

- Do some of the skill lessons together to help students develop strategies for selecting answers and for different types of questions. Use the "clues" for learning strategies for test taking.

- Make certain that students know how to mark a separate answer sheet. Use the practice test and answer sheet so that they are familiar with the process.

- Review the directions for each test. Identify key words that students must use to answer the questions. Do the sample test questions with the class.

- Remind students to answer each question, to budget their time so they can complete all the questions, and to apply strategies for determining answers.

Reduce the mystery of taking tests for your students. By using *Spectrum Test Practice*, you have the materials that show them what the tests will look like, what kinds of questions are on the tests, and ways to help them be more successful taking tests.

Note: The reading comprehension questions in all selections are in the same order: main idea, recalling details/sequencing, inferencing/drawing conclusions, fact and opinion/cause and effect, and story elements. This information can be used to diagnose areas for needed instruction.

Note: If you wish to time your students on a practice test, we suggest allowing 1.09 minutes per question for this grade level.

Dear Parent/Guardian:

We will be giving tests to measure your child's learning. These tests include questions that relate to the information your child is learning in school. The tests may be standardized and used throughout the nation, or they may be specific to our state. Regardless of the test, the results are used to measure student achievement.

Many students do not test well even though they know the material. They may not test well because of test anxiety or the mystery of taking tests. What will the test look like? What will some of the questions be? What happens if I do not do well?

To help your child do his/her best on the tests, we will be using some practice tests. These tests help your child learn what the tests will look like, what some of the questions might be, and ways to learn to take tests. These practice tests will be included as part of your child's homework.

You can help your child with this important part of learning. Below are some suggestions:

- Ask your child if he/she has homework.
- Provide a quiet place to work.
- Go over the work with your child.
- Use a timer to help your child learn to manage his/her time when taking tests.
- Tell your child he/she is doing a good job.
- Remind him/her to use the clues that are included in the lessons.

If your child is having difficulty with the tests, these ideas may be helpful:

- Review the examples.
- Skip the difficult questions and come back to them later.
- Guess at those that you do not know.
- Answer all the questions.

By showing you are interested in how your child is doing, he/she will do even better in school. Enjoy this time with your child. Good luck with the practice tests.

Sincerely,

Sample Standards	Spectrum Test Practice Gr. 6	*CAT Level for Gr. 6	**CTBS Level for Gr. 6	Other	Other	Other
Reading						
Vocabulary						
Understanding Figurative Language		X	X			
Using Common Foreign Words	X					
Using Context Clues	X	X	X			
Understanding Slight Differences in Meaning	X		X			
Using Synonyms and Antonyms	X		X			
Using Multi-Meaning Words	X		X			
Using Common Roots and Word Parts	X		X			
Comprehension						
Identifying Main Idea	X	X	X			
Using Graphic Organizers		X	X			
Comparing and Contrasting	X	X	X			
Reading Various Genre	X	X	X			
Summarizing	X	X	X			
Using Popular Media	X					
Identifying Author's Purpose	X		X			
Distinguishing Between Fact and Opinion	X	X	X			
Identifying Character Traits/Feelings	X		X			
Identifying Supporting Details	X	X	X			
Identifying the Speaker	X					
Understanding Literary Devices			X			
Understanding Themes	X	X	X			
Identifying Cause and Effect	X	X	X			
Drawing Conclusions	X	X	X			
Using Context Clues	X	X	X			
Language						
Mechanics						
Expression						
Using Graphic Organizers		X	X			
Understanding Purpose	X	X	X			
Using Topic Sentences	X	X	X			
Using Supporting Sentences for Paragraphs	X	X	X			
Drawing Logical Conclusions	X	X	X			
Using Editing Skills		X	X			
Using Different Types of Writing	X	X	X			
Using Simple, Compound, and Complex Sentences	X	X	X			
Using Proper Grammar	X	X	X			
Using Correct Capitalization and Punctuation	X	X	X			
Spelling						
Identifying Correct Spelling	X		X			
Identifying Incorrect Spelling	X		X			

* Terra Nova CAT™   ©2001 CTB/McGraw-Hill
** Terra Nova CTBS®   ©1997 CTB/McGraw-Hill

CORRELATION TO STANDARDS

● **Grade 6**

Sample Standards	Spectrum Test Practice Gr. 6	*CAT Level for Gr. 6	**CTBS Level for Gr. 6	Other	Other	Other
Study Skills						
Using Reference Materials	X		X			
Math						
Concepts						
Numeration						
Comparing and Ordering Positive and Negative Integers	X	X	X			
Comparing and Ordering Fractions, Decimals, Percents	X					
Using Number Lines	X		X			
Renaming Numbers	X		X			
Finding Least Common Multiple	X	X				
Finding Greatest Common Factor	X	X				
Recognizing Decimal-Fraction Equivalents	X					
Recognizing Patterns		X	X			
Using Models	X	X	X			
Understanding Place Value	X		X			
Understanding Greater Than and Less Than	X	X	X			
Understanding Odd and Even Numbers	X					
Understanding Prime and Composite Numbers	X					
Computation						
Using Operations on the Set of Integers	X	X	X			
Using Operations on Fractions, Decimals, Percents	X	X	X			
Using Rounding of Numbers	X		X			
Using Ratio	X	X	X			
Using Probability	X	X	X			
Calculating Percentages	X		X			
Using Estimation	X	X	X			
Using Mental Arithmetic		X	X			
Using Appropriate Operations	X					
Algebra and Functions						
Using Equations	X	X	X			
Using Formulas	X	X	X			
Using Variables	X					
Geometry						
Identifying Properties of Lines and Angles	X	X	X			
Identifying Similar Two-Dimensional Shapes	X		X			
Understanding Symmetry and Congruency	X	X	X			
Identifying Two-Dimensional Shapes	X	X	X			
Identifying Geometric Solids	X					
Measurement						
Using Standard Units and Tools to Measure	X	X	X			
Comparing Different Units of Measure	X	X	X			
Calculating Circumference						

* Terra Nova CAT™ ©2001 CTB/McGraw-Hill
** Terra Nova CTBS® ©1997 CTB/McGraw-Hill

Published by Spectrum. Copyright protected.

Published by Spectrum. Copyright protected.

● Grade 6

Sample Standards	Spectrum Test Practice Gr. 6	*CAT Level for Gr. 6	**CTBS Level for Gr. 6	Other	Other	Other
Measurement (cont.)						
Calculating Area	X	X	X			
Calculating Amounts of Money	X	X	X			
Understanding Time and Elapsed Time	X		X			
Understanding Volume	X		X			
Understanding Perimeter	X					
Data Analysis						
Probability						
Graphing Data	X	X	X			
Understanding Averages (Mean, Median, Mode)			X			
Using Data to Predict Future Events			X			
Problem Solving						
Identifying Relevant and Irrelevant Information	X		X			
Using Strategies to Solve Problems	X	X	X			
Estimating Results	X	X	X			
Recognizing Reasonable Solutions	X	X	X			
Science						
Understanding the Solar System	X	X				
Understanding the Earth	X	X	X			
Understanding the Sun	X					
Understanding the Environment	X	X	X			
Understanding Matter and Energy	X	X	X			
Understanding Electricity and Circuits	X	X	X			
Understanding Plants and Animals	X	X	X			
Understanding Plant and Animal Classification	X	X	X			
Understanding the Human Body	X	X	X			
Social Studies						
Understanding Ancient Civilizations and Events	X	X	X			
History						
Understanding the Interconnection of People		X	X			
Understanding the History of Spain						
Understanding the Histories of Mexico and South America	X					
Government						
Comparing Governments		X	X			
Economics						
Understanding International Trade and Currencies			X			
Understanding and Comparing Economic Issues		X	X			
Understanding Savings and Investments						
Geography						
Interpreting Maps	X	X	X			
Identifying the States of Mexico	X					
Identifying the Provinces of Canada	X		X			
Identifying Countries and Cities in Europe	X					

* Terra Nova CAT™ ©2001 CTB/McGraw-Hill
** Terra Nova CTBS® ©1997 CTB/McGraw-Hill

READING: VOCABULARY

Lesson 1: Synonyms

Directions: Read each item. Choose the answer that means the same or about the same as the underlined word. Fill in the circle for the correct answer.

Examples

A. **cheap** gift
- (A) generous
- (B) stingy
- (C) expensive
- (D) charitable

B. A **frank** answer is —
- (F) short
- (G) honest
- (H) long
- (J) complicated

 Clue Look carefully at all the answer choices.

Practice

1. **tiresome** job
- (A) hurried
- (B) slow
- (C) tedious
- (D) dim

2. **arrogant** man
- (F) heavy
- (G) proud
- (H) cunning
- (J) humble

3. **surly** individual
- (A) wild
- (B) anxious
- (C) gruff
- (D) calm

4. **agile** body
- (F) clumsy
- (G) heavy
- (H) nimble
- (J) thin

5. To be in the **midst** is to be in the —
- (A) center
- (B) dark
- (C) crowd
- (D) outskirts

6. A person in **peril** is in —
- (F) clothing
- (G) safety
- (H) luck
- (J) danger

7. To **thrive** is to —
- (A) withdraw
- (B) wither
- (C) prosper
- (D) participate

8. An **ally** is a —
- (F) metal
- (G) friend
- (H) neighbor
- (J) enemy

STOP

READING: VOCABULARY

● Lesson 2: Vocabulary Skills

Directions: Read each item. Choose the answer that means the same or about the same as the underlined word. Fill in the circle for the correct answer.

Examples

A. A diminutive woman
- (A) tiny
- (B) industrious
- (C) slow
- (D) energetic

B. It was an ambush. Ambush means —
- (F) a courageous fight
- (G) a surprise attack
- (H) a change in plans
- (J) a flowering plant

 Clue If a question is too difficult, skip it and come back to it later.

● Practice

1. Prolong the agony
- (A) stretch
- (B) shorten
- (C) stop
- (D) postpone

2. Scour the tub
- (F) preserve
- (G) fill
- (H) scrub
- (J) lug

3. Unruly behavior
- (A) ridiculous
- (B) obedient
- (C) calm
- (D) willful

4. Concealed the evidence
- (F) avoided
- (G) revealed
- (H) hidden
- (J) examined

5. Her bias was plain to see. Bias means —
- (A) point of view
- (B) loss
- (C) wisdom
- (D) slip

6. The boy had a hunch. A hunch is a —
- (F) feeling
- (G) bad attitude
- (H) hump
- (J) cramp

7. The professor rambled. Rambled means —
- (A) to get lost
- (B) babbled
- (C) argued
- (D) stopped

8. The twins mustered their courage. Mustered means —
- (F) lost
- (G) faked
- (H) proclaimed
- (J) gathered

STOP

READING: VOCABULARY

Lesson 3: Antonyms

Directions: Read each item. Choose the word that means the opposite of the underlined word. Fill in the circle for the correct answer.

Examples

A. <u>willing</u> to leave
- (A) able
- (B) eager
- (C) reluctant
- (D) allowed

B. <u>simple</u> room
- (F) ornate
- (G) empty
- (H) full
- (J) unusual

 Clue If you are not sure which answer is correct, take your best guess. Eliminate answers that mean the same thing as the underlined word.

Practice

1. <u>dissimilar</u> answers
   - (A) identical
   - (B) strange
   - (C) unusual
   - (D) unlike

2. The play <u>commenced</u>.
   - (F) concluded
   - (G) began
   - (H) continued
   - (J) failed

3. <u>benign</u> host
   - (A) kind
   - (B) spiteful
   - (C) young
   - (D) gracious

4. opened <u>gingerly</u>
   - (F) carefully
   - (G) carelessly
   - (H) swiftly
   - (J) gradually

5. <u>absurd</u> situation
   - (A) ridiculous
   - (B) horrible
   - (C) funny
   - (D) sensible

6. <u>hoist</u> the sails
   - (F) lift
   - (G) lower
   - (H) display
   - (J) mend

7. <u>vacant</u> room
   - (A) clean
   - (B) ancient
   - (C) empty
   - (D) inhabited

8. <u>motivated</u> worker
   - (F) energized
   - (G) uninspired
   - (H) roused
   - (J) new

STOP

READING: VOCABULARY

● Lesson 4: Multi-Meaning Words

Directions: Read the directions carefully. For items A, 1, and 2, choose the correct answer. For items B, 3, and 4, choose the word that fits in both sentences.

Examples

A. Because of her fever, she felt faint. In which sentence does the word faint mean the same thing as in the sentence above?

- Ⓐ Her dress was a faint pink.
- Ⓑ When he saw the blood, he felt faint.
- Ⓒ The writing on the yellowing paper was very faint.
- Ⓓ Her voice was so faint I could barely hear it.

B. Did someone _____ the cookies?

Leather is the _____ of an animal.

- Ⓕ eat
- Ⓖ hide
- Ⓗ skin
- Ⓙ bake

 Clue Use the meaning of the sentences to find the right answer. Check your answer again before you fill in the circle.

● Practice

1. Will you brush my hair? In which sentence does the word brush mean the same thing as in the sentence above?
   - Ⓐ She bought a new brush.
   - Ⓑ After the storm, the yard was littered with brush.
   - Ⓒ I need to brush the dog.
   - Ⓓ She felt the kitten brush against her leg.

2. He plans to store the corn in his barn. In which sentence does the word store mean the same thing as in the sentence above?
   - Ⓕ She went to the grocery store.
   - Ⓖ My dad will store the lawn mower in the shed.
   - Ⓗ The owner will store his shelves with merchandise.
   - Ⓙ My favorite store is in the mall.

3. The _____ piece goes here. The first _____ of the tournament is over.
   - Ⓐ square
   - Ⓑ part
   - Ⓒ round
   - Ⓓ circular

4. The second _____ of our encyclopedia set is missing. Please turn down the _____ on your stereo.
   - Ⓕ sound
   - Ⓖ volume
   - Ⓗ book
   - Ⓙ dial

STOP

Name _____ Date_____

READING: VOCABULARY

● **Lesson 5: Words in Context**

Directions: Read the paragraph. Find the word that fits best in each numbered blank. Fill in the circle for the correct answer.

Examples

Ashley was _____ **(A)** when she won the honor of representing her school in the spelling bee. This annual event gave students the opportunity to represent their schools in a statewide competition. Ashley could hardly wait. The winner would be _____ **(B)** the state champion.

A.
- (A) disappointed
- (B) indifferent
- (C) bothered
- (D) delighted

B.
- (F) declared
- (G) invited
- (H) justified
- (J) deceived

Clue If you aren't sure which answer is correct, substitute each answer in the blank.

● **Practice**

People who travel or cross the Amazon and Orinoco Rivers of South America are careful never to _____ **(1)** a foot or hand from the side of their boat. For just below the surface of these mighty waters _____ **(2)** a small fish feared throughout the _____ **(3)**. That fish is the flesh-eating piranha. It has a nasty _____ **(4)** and an even nastier _____ **(5)**. Although smaller fish make up most of its diet, the piranha will _____ **(6)** both humans and other animals.

1.
- (A) lift
- (B) dangle
- (C) withdraw
- (D) brush

2.
- (F) lurks
- (G) nests
- (H) plays
- (J) boasts

3.
- (A) universe
- (B) town
- (C) continent
- (D) village

4.
- (F) habit
- (G) friend
- (H) flavor
- (J) disposition

5.
- (A) smile
- (B) brother
- (C) appetite
- (D) memory

6.
- (F) befriend
- (G) bully
- (H) attack
- (J) analyze

STOP

READING: VOCABULARY

● **Lesson 6: Word Study**

Directions: Read each question. Fill in the circle for the correct answer.

Examples

A. Which of these words probably comes from the Spanish word *chaparro* meaning "evergreen oak"?

- Ⓐ chapel
- Ⓑ chaparral
- Ⓒ chaplain
- Ⓓ chapter

B. Golden retrievers _____ children well.

Which of these words would indicate that golden retrievers get along well with children?

- Ⓕ reject
- Ⓖ tolerate
- Ⓗ display
- Ⓙ manipulate

 Clue Stay with your first answer. It is more often right than it is wrong.

● **Practice**

1. Eggs are to omelet as bread is to _____.
   - Ⓐ lunch
   - Ⓑ sandwich
   - Ⓒ wheat
   - Ⓓ cheese

2. Which of these words probably comes from the Greek *gumnastes* meaning "athletic trainer"?
   - Ⓕ gumption
   - Ⓖ gymnast
   - Ⓗ gumshoe
   - Ⓙ gusto

3. Carlos did not want to _____.
   Which word means "to interfere"?
   - Ⓐ interval
   - Ⓑ insult
   - Ⓒ intrude
   - Ⓓ surpass

4. The sailors _____ their water supplies.
   Which word means the sailors "refilled" their water supplies?
   - Ⓕ detected
   - Ⓖ allocated
   - Ⓗ participated
   - Ⓙ replenished

For numbers 5 and 6, choose the answer that best defines the underlined part.

5. pri<u>mer</u>   pri<u>meval</u>
   - Ⓐ elementary
   - Ⓑ original
   - Ⓒ first
   - Ⓓ former

6. <u>cour</u>ier   <u>cours</u>er
   - Ⓕ running
   - Ⓖ ruling
   - Ⓗ coursing
   - Ⓙ turning

STOP

Name _____   Date_____

READING: VOCABULARY
SAMPLE TEST

● **Directions:** For items E1 and 1–8, choose the word or words that mean the same or almost the same as the underlined word. For item E2, fill in the circle for the correct answer.

Examples

E1. **possessed** information
- Ⓐ questioned
- Ⓑ discovered
- Ⓒ had
- Ⓓ lost

E2. **Which of these words probably comes from the Greek word *horama* meaning "sight."**
- Ⓕ orangutan
- Ⓖ panorama
- Ⓗ amazing
- Ⓙ amass

---

1. important **data**
- Ⓐ computer
- Ⓑ meeting
- Ⓒ information
- Ⓓ announcement

2. **promptly** returned
- Ⓕ quickly
- Ⓖ quietly
- Ⓗ hesitantly
- Ⓙ gallantly

3. **emphatic** reply
- Ⓐ humorous
- Ⓑ forceful
- Ⓒ emotional
- Ⓓ weak

4. huge **commotion**
- Ⓕ noise
- Ⓖ concert
- Ⓗ disturbance
- Ⓙ crowd

5. To **urge** someone is to —
- Ⓐ encourage
- Ⓑ discourage
- Ⓒ invite
- Ⓓ conceal

6. To **crouch** is to —
- Ⓕ crawl
- Ⓖ jump up
- Ⓗ stoop
- Ⓙ shrink

7. **Gnarled** means —
- Ⓐ grumpy
- Ⓑ knotted
- Ⓒ lifelike
- Ⓓ smooth

8. If someone is **bewildered**, he is —
- Ⓕ enchanted
- Ⓖ enlightened
- Ⓗ confused
- Ⓙ correct

GO ON

9. Her description was <u>precise</u>.
   To be precise is to be —
   - (A) specific
   - (B) inaccurate
   - (C) imaginative
   - (D) peculiar

10. Heather was <u>chagrined</u>.
    To be chagrined is to be —
    - (F) happy
    - (G) embarrassed
    - (H) angry
    - (J) enthusiastic

11. The brothers had to <u>fend</u> for themselves.
    To fend is to —
    - (A) manage
    - (B) discover
    - (C) shop
    - (D) reply

12. She had an airtight <u>alibi</u>.
    Alibi means —
    - (F) raft
    - (G) excuse
    - (H) opinion
    - (J) claim

13. It was a clever <u>device</u>.
    Device means —
    - (A) gadget
    - (B) announcement
    - (C) trap
    - (D) development

For numbers 14–19, choose the word that means the opposite of the underlined word.

14. a ship <u>adrift</u>
    - (F) sinking
    - (G) floating
    - (H) anchored
    - (J) lost

15. <u>rouse</u> someone
    - (A) awaken
    - (B) anger
    - (C) soothe
    - (D) enliven

16. good <u>chum</u>
    - (F) quality
    - (G) deed
    - (H) friend
    - (J) stranger

17. <u>acute</u> pain
    - (A) intense
    - (B) sharp
    - (C) intermittent
    - (D) dull

18. eat with <u>relish</u>
    - (F) enjoyment
    - (G) disgust
    - (H) zest
    - (J) pleasure

19. <u>outlandish</u> clothing
    - (A) outrageous
    - (B) peculiar
    - (C) ordinary
    - (D) ridiculous

GO ON

Name _____ Date_____

For numbers 20–23, choose the word that correctly completes both sentences.

20. **Please hand me a _____.**

    She needed a _____ transplant.

    - (F) kidney
    - (G) hand
    - (H) tissue
    - (J) hammer

21. **That was _____.**

    There were an _____ number of players.

    - (A) strange
    - (B) odd
    - (C) quick
    - (D) outside

22. **The stars _____ at night.**

    You _____ to be ill.

    - (F) seem
    - (G) pretend
    - (H) appear
    - (J) shine

23. **What's all that _____?**

    He hit the ball with his _____.

    - (A) noise
    - (B) bat
    - (C) commotion
    - (D) racket

24. **I don't recognize your <u>accent</u>.**

    In which sentence does the word <u>accent</u> mean the same thing as in the sentence above?

    - (F) Place the <u>accent</u> above the second syllable.
    - (G) You forgot to include the <u>accent</u> mark.
    - (H) She has a southern <u>accent</u>.
    - (J) There is an <u>accent</u> on reading programs.

25. **The directions were very <u>complex</u>.**

    In which sentence does the word <u>complex</u> mean the same thing as in the sentence above?

    - (A) Alicia had a spider <u>complex</u>.
    - (B) This map is too <u>complex</u> for me.
    - (C) What's a <u>complex</u> carbohydrate?
    - (D) They lived in an apartment <u>complex</u>.

For numbers 26 and 27, choose the answer that best defines the underlined part.

26. <u>man</u>ual   <u>man</u>uscript

    - (F) hand
    - (G) write
    - (H) dictate
    - (J) instead of

27. <u>mis</u>treat   <u>mis</u>pronounce

    - (A) almost
    - (B) badly
    - (C) not
    - (D) opposite of

GO ON

Name _____ Date_____

READING: VOCABULARY
SAMPLE TEST (cont.)

28. Which of these words probably comes from the Old French word *aaisier* meaning "to put at ease"?

- (F) simple
- (G) easy
- (H) aisle
- (J) alas

29. Which of these words probably comes from the Latin word *ferox* meaning "fierce"?

- (A) ferret
- (B) ferment
- (C) ferocious
- (D) fervor

30. The design was very _____.
Which of these words means "elaborate"?

- (F) intrepid
- (G) serviceable
- (H) intricate
- (J) exclusive

31. They gave _____ to the officer.
Which of these words means "to give honor to" the officer?

- (A) homage
- (B) flourish
- (C) ballast
- (D) image

Read the paragraph. Choose the word below the paragraph that fits best in each numbered blank.

Laughter is good medicine. Scientists believe that laughter _____ (32) the heart and lungs. Laughter burns calories and may help _____ (33) blood pressure. It also _____ (34) stress and tension. If you are _____ (35) about an upcoming test, laughter can help you relax.

32.
- (F) heals
- (G) stresses
- (H) weakens
- (J) strengthens

33.
- (A) raise
- (B) lower
- (C) eliminate
- (D) elongate

34.
- (F) relieves
- (G) increases
- (H) revives
- (J) releases

35.
- (A) excited
- (B) enthusiastic
- (C) nervous
- (D) knowledgeable

STOP

READING: READING COMPREHENSION

● **Lesson 7: Main Idea**

Directions: Read the passage. Choose the best answer to each question. Fill in the circle for the answer of your choice.

Example

The experts are not always right. They advised the big mining companies to pass up the Cripple Creek region. They claimed that no gold could be found there. It was left up to local prospectors to uncover the incredible wealth of Cripple Creek. More than $400 million worth of ore was found in this area that experts ignored.

A. What is the paragraph mainly about?
- Ⓐ what experts thought about Cripple Creek
- Ⓑ when gold was found at Cripple Creek
- Ⓒ how much the ore was worth
- Ⓓ how big mining companies operate

 Clue If a question sounds confusing, try to restate it in simpler terms. Be sure you understand the question before you choose an answer.

● **Practice**

The practice of wearing rings is a very ancient one. Throughout history, people in many lands have decorated their bodies by wearing rings on their fingers, ears, lips, necks, noses, ankles, and wrists. In some cultures, a married woman wore a ring on the big toe of her left foot; a man might have put rings on his second and third toes. Today, the practice of wearing rings in some cases includes multiple facial rings, as well as rings in many other areas of the body.

1. What is the paragraph mainly about?
- Ⓐ why some people wore rings on their toes
- Ⓑ what kinds of rings were the most popular
- Ⓒ when the practice of wearing rings began
- Ⓓ how people throughout history have worn rings

2. Which title best summarizes this passage?
- Ⓕ Rings Worn Today
- Ⓖ Rings Throughout the Ages
- Ⓗ Rings in Unusual Places
- Ⓙ Rings Are Fun

 STOP

READING: READING COMPREHENSION

● **Lesson 8: Recalling Details**

Directions: Read the passage. Choose the best answer to each question. Fill in the circle for the answer of your choice.

Example

The frankfurter, named for the city of Frankfurt, Germany, is easily the most popular sausage in the world. Frankfurters, popularly known as "hot dogs," are sold almost everywhere in the United States. They are consumed in great quantities at sporting events and amusement parks. People from other countries often associate hot dogs with the American way of life.

A. Where are huge numbers of hot dogs eaten?

- Ⓐ in Frankfurt, Germany
- Ⓑ in other countries
- Ⓒ at sporting events
- Ⓓ in stores

Look for key words in the question, and then find the same or similar words in the passage. This will help you locate the correct answer.

● **Practice**

Around the year 370 B.C., the Greek philosopher Plato wrote about a huge continent that once existed in the Atlantic Ocean. Plato called the continent Atlantis and stated that it was approximately the size of Europe. Atlantis was supposedly the home of a mighty nation with powerful armies that had subdued parts of Europe and North Africa.

Plato's account of Atlantis came from his research of the records of an earlier Athenian ruler named Solon. Solon was supposed to have visited Egypt several hundred years before, and it was there that he heard about Atlantis.

Atlantis was said to have beautiful cities with advanced technologies. The climate was so ideal that two growing seasons were possible. The land teemed with herbs, fruits, and other plants and was the habitat of many

animals. Life was good until, according to Plato, the citizens of Atlantis became greedy and incurred the wrath of the gods. Then great earthquakes and floods that continued nonstop for a day and night caused the continent to sink into the ocean.

1. Who was Plato?

- Ⓐ a citizen of Atlantis
- Ⓑ a philosopher
- Ⓒ a ruler
- Ⓓ a warrior

2. Where did Plato believe the continent of Atlantis was located?

- Ⓕ near Egypt
- Ⓖ in the Pacific Ocean
- Ⓗ in the Atlantic Ocean
- Ⓙ in the North Sea

READING: READING COMPREHENSION

● **Lesson 9: Drawing Conclusions**

Directions: Read the passage. Choose the best answer to each question. Fill in the circle for the answer of your choice.

Example

English women once thought they looked best with wigs that rose two or even three feet above their heads. It certainly made them look taller. Wool, cotton, and goats' hair were used to give the hairpieces the desired height. The finest high-piled wigs were often decorated with imitation fruit, model ships, horses, and figurines.

A. **From the story you cannot tell —**
- (A) the color of the wigs
- (B) the height of the wigs
- (C) what the wigs were made of
- (D) how wigs were decorated

 Skim the passage so you have an understanding of what it is about. Then skim the questions. Answer the easiest questions first, then look back at the passage to find the answers.

● **Practice**

I'll admit the list is long. I broke Mom's favorite blue vase playing baseball in the house. It was a home run, but that didn't count much with Mom. I broke the back window. I didn't think I could break a window by shoving my hip against a door. It must have been bad glass. I ruined the living room carpet by leaving a red spot the size of a basketball. I know the rule—no drinking in the living room—but I wasn't really drinking. I didn't even get a sip before I dropped the glass.

I guess "Trouble" is my middle name. At least that's what Mom says. So you won't be surprised when I tell you I'm in trouble once again.

1. **What is the main problem in the story?**
- (A) The narrator drinks red pop in the living room.
- (B) The narrator breaks and destroys things.
- (C) The narrator disobeys the rules.
- (D) The narrator is in trouble again.

2. **What do you think happens next in the story?**
- (F) The narrator gets a paper route to pay for all the damages.
- (G) The narrator apologizes for ruining the carpet.
- (H) The narrator tells about the latest trouble he caused.
- (J) The narrator asks for a new middle name.

 GO ON

● **Lesson 9: Drawing Conclusions (cont.)**

Directions: Read the passage. Choose the best answer to each question. Fill in the circle for the answer of your choice.

Example

By actually fishing for and catching other fish, the anglerfish grows to be almost four feet long. It lies quietly in mud at the bottom of the water. Three wormlike "fingers" on the top of its head attract other fish. When the fish come close, the anglerfish gets its meal. If fishing is slow, the anglerfish may rise to the surface and swallow ducks, loons, or even geese.

B. From this passage, what can you conclude about anglerfish?

(F) Anglerfish prefer fish to other animals.

(G) They have worms growing out of their heads.

(H) Birds often eat anglerfish.

(J) They always remain at the bottom of the water.

Skip crossed only one set of fingers when he made a wish. He avoided black cats and never stepped on cracks in the sidewalk. He thought he was a perfect candidate to win something, anything.

Skip knew that winning took more than avoiding cracks and black cats. That's why he tried out for the track team. Skip wanted to hear the words, "You are the winner!" He imagined hearing his name announced over the loud speaker. However, Skip didn't work very hard at practice and didn't make the team.

Skip spent his free time kicking stones down the street. He pretended he was an NFL kicker in a championship game. The score was always 0–0, and his kick would cinch the title. In his imagination, he always scored.

Skip believed he would be a football star when he grew up. He decided it didn't matter that he hadn't made the track team. He would play football when he got to high school. He was such a great kicker; he would easily make

the team. He might even play in college, he thought. He really wanted to be a winner.

3. Which sentence best summarizes this story?

(A) Skip was very superstitious.

(B) Skip really wanted to be a winner.

(C) Skip had a vivid imagination.

(D) Track was not the right sport for Skip.

4. Which sentence best describes what Skip will need to do to be a winner?

(F) Skip will need to stop being so superstitious.

(G) Skip will need to work hard to succeed.

(H) Skip will need to find someone to coach him.

(J) Skip will need to stop kicking stones.

STOP

READING: READING COMPREHENSION

● Lesson 10: Fact and Opinion & Cause and Effect

Directions: Read the passage. Choose the best answer to each question. Fill in the circle for the answer of your choice.

Example

The shellfish shrimp is a popular food. Shrimp are found in both fresh and salt water. Most shrimp have five pairs of thin front legs and five pairs of back legs. The front legs are used for walking and the back legs for swimming. Unlike most animals, if a shrimp damages or loses a leg, it can grow a new one.

A. Which sentence below is an opinion, not a fact?

(A) Shrimp can grow new legs.

(B) Shrimp live in fresh and salt water.

(C) Shrimp prefer to walk, not swim.

(D) Shrimp have five pairs of front legs.

 Clue   Skim the passage for facts. Remember: Facts can be proven.

● Practice

Jessica and Suzanne were friends and neighbors. They loved to solve mysteries so much that they began their own club, the Mystery Solvers Club.

One Saturday p.m., the day of their weekly meeting, Suzanne went to her room at 2:00 to get her journal. It was missing! The journal contained all the information and all the notes from each of the club's meetings and cases. Suzanne ran to the meeting place in Jessica's backyard. Suzanne exclaimed, "My journal is missing! You must help me find it."

The club members were concerned. They needed the club notes to solve a mystery from the week before. Jessica said, "Tell us all you know."

Suzanne replied, "I keep the journal in the drawer of my bedside table. Last night I was writing in it while I ate a sandwich. I don't remember much else except that I was very tired. I didn't think about my journal again until just now. It wasn't in my drawer where I keep it."

1. Which sentence below is not a fact?

(A) The club met on Saturday.

(B) Jessica and Suzanne were friends.

(C) Suzanne went to her room at 2:00 to get the journal.

(D) Someone took Suzanne's journal.

2. Because Suzanne has lost her journal, what will the club members probably do next?

(F) The club will buy a new journal.

(G) They will search for the missing journal.

(H) They will move on to the next mystery.

(J) Suzanne and Jessica will no longer be friends.

 STOP

READING: READING COMPREHENSION

● **Lesson 11: Story Elements**

Directions: Read the passage. Choose the best answer to each question. Fill in the circle for the answer of your choice.

Example

The space taxi's engine hummed. Nathan's teeth chattered. Little wells of moisture beaded up on his forehead and palms. *I can't fly*, he thought. *Mars is just around the corner, but it's still too far to be stuck in this taxi.* Nathan knew that his uncle was waiting for him, waiting for help with his hydroponic farm. At first, that didn't matter. In his mind, Nathan saw himself leaping out of his seat and bolting toward the door. But then he thought of his uncle. Nathan knew that if he did not help his uncle, the crops he had worked so hard to nurture and grow would not be ready for the Mars 3 season. He took a deep breath and settled back for the remainder of the flight. He couldn't wait to see the look on his uncle's face when he stepped off the taxi.

A.   What is the setting of this story?
- (A) Earth
- (B) a space farm
- (C) a space taxi
- (D) unknown

Clue Read the passage quickly for clues to the setting and problem.

● **Practice**

"What do you wanna play?" Will asked as he shoved a bite of pancake into his mouth.

"Scramble. We are Scramble maniacs at this house," said Scott.

Will poured more orange juice into his glass. "How about that game where you ask dumb questions about stuff everyone always forgets?"

"Trivial Questions," said Scott.

"Yeah, that's it."

"Can you name the seven dwarfs?" asked Eric.

"Snoopy, Sneezy, Dopey," said Scott.

"Nah, Snoopy's a dog," said Eric.

"Let's do something else," Will chimed in as he cut his pancake in half.

"Let's play Scramble," said Scott.

"That's too much like school. Let's play football," said Eric.

"It's too cold out," said Scott.

"Let's dig out your connector sets. I haven't played with those for years," Eric said as he pushed his chair back and stood.

"Yeah," said Scott and Will as they jumped from their seats.

1.   What is the setting for this story?
- (A) Scott's bedroom
- (B) Scott's living room
- (C) Scott's kitchen
- (D) Scott's basement

2.   What is the problem in this story?
- (F) The boys cannot remember the names of the seven dwarfs.
- (G) The boys cannot decide what they want to do.
- (H) The boys do not want to play Scramble.
- (J) It's too cold to play football.

26

═══════ READING: READING COMPREHENSION ═══════

● Lesson 12: Fiction

Directions: Read the passage. Choose the best answer to each question. Fill in the circle for the answer of your choice.

Example

Excited, the guinea pig squealed with delight when the girl entered the room. Surely the girl would give her a special treat. Instead, the girl threw herself down on the bed. "It's not fair," the girl said. Disappointed, the guinea pig closed her eyes and went back to sleep.

A.   What title best summarizes this story?

- Ⓐ Squeals of Delight
- Ⓑ A Guinea Pig's Perspective
- Ⓒ The Sad Girl
- Ⓓ A Special Treat

 Skim the passage so you have an understanding of what it is about. Then skim the questions. Answer the easiest questions first, and then look back to the passage to find the answers.

● Practice

"You said there was a river near here. Why don't we go swimming?" suggested Mara, wiping the sweat off her brow.

"Oh, you wouldn't want to swim in that river!" said Eva.

"Why not?" Mara asked. "I'm a strong swimmer. Even if the river's deep or the current's fast, it won't bother me."

"It's not that the river is deep or fast," said Eva. "If you like swimming with tires, broken bottles, and rusty cans, you can swim there."

"Well," said Mara, "I don't think I want to swim that badly. Unless—isn't there a public pool in town?"

1.   Why did Mara probably want to go swimming?

- Ⓐ It was a warm day.
- Ⓑ Mara felt daring.
- Ⓒ The girls were bored.
- Ⓓ It was raining out.

2.   What will the girls most likely do next?

- Ⓕ visit a friend
- Ⓖ go swimming in a pool
- Ⓗ swim in the river
- Ⓙ go back to Eva's house

READING: READING COMPREHENSION

● Lesson 13: Fiction

Directions: Read the passage. Choose the best answer to each question. Fill in the circle for the answer of your choice.

Example

"We're out of eggs, Sis," Willis complained. "We can't make supper."

"I was afraid we might be," said Sis. "On cold days like today, Mom usually stops at Phil's Diner on her way home from work for a cup of hot coffee. Let's call the diner and leave a message for her." Sis dialed the diner.

An hour later, Mom came home with a bag of groceries but no eggs.

A.   What can we conclude from the last paragraph?

- Ⓐ   Mom decided not to buy eggs.
- Ⓑ   Mom went shopping instead of stopping at the diner.
- Ⓒ   Willis discovered eggs in the back of the refrigerator.
- Ⓓ   Mom had a dozen eggs in her bag of groceries.

Clue Skim the passage so you have an understanding of what it is about. Then skim the questions. Answer the easiest questions first, and then look back to the passage to find the answers.

● Practice

The Special Gift

T.J. was poised to take a bite of his birthday cake when his mother said, "Not so fast, Mister. I think you have one more present coming."

"Really? What is it?" T.J. asked.

His father rose from his seat and walked around to T.J.'s chair. "Son, I have been waiting for this day to give you a very special gift. My father gave it to me when I was about your age, and it has been one of my most valued possessions. Now I want to give it to you." He then placed an old, dusty shoebox tied with string in front of T.J.

"This is my stamp collection, Son," his father began. "Your grandfather and I worked on it together. Now I want you to have it. I'll teach you about the different stamps and how to preserve them. We can go to the post office tomorrow after school, and you can pick out one of the new stamp sets to add to your collection."

T.J. tried to be excited about his gift, but he didn't understand what was so great about a box of old stamps. "Thanks, Dad," he said with a forced smile.

GO ON

READING: READING COMPREHENSION

● Lesson 13: Fiction (cont.)

Then he noticed that Felicia had taken the box and was looking in each of the envelopes inside. "Look at this one!" she exclaimed. "It's from the year I was born. Hey, T.J., here's one from the year you were born, too!"

"That's right," said T.J.'s grandfather. "There are even stamps from my birthday!"

T.J. began to understand why the box was so important to his father and grandfather. He moved close to Felicia so that he could see the stamps better. Twenty minutes later, he didn't even notice that his ice cream was melted all over his cake.

1. **What is the main idea of this story?**
   - (A) Good manners are best.
   - (B) T.J. received a very special gift.
   - (C) Stamps are valuable.
   - (D) It's the thought that counts.

2. **When Felicia discovers the stamps from the years she and T.J. were born, what does T.J. begin to understand?**
   - (F) He and Felicia are about the same age.
   - (G) Some of the stamps are older than he is.
   - (H) The stamps are very meaningful.
   - (J) He was born after the collection was begun.

3. **Why didn't T.J. notice that his ice cream was melting?**
   - (A) He was no longer hungry.
   - (B) He was interested in the stamps.
   - (C) He did not like chocolate ice cream.
   - (D) He had already left the table.

4. **Which of these sentences is an opinion?**
   - (F) The stamp collection was very special to T.J.'s dad.
   - (G) At first, T.J. did not understand why the gift was so special.
   - (H) Collecting stamps is boring.
   - (J) Some of the stamps were very old.

5. **Who is the main character in this story?**
   - (A) Grandfather
   - (B) T.J.
   - (C) Father
   - (D) Felicia

6. **In the sentence, "I'll teach you about the different stamps and how to preserve them," the word *preserve* probably means —**
   - (F) to keep in good condition
   - (G) to store
   - (H) to sell to make money
   - (J) to keep from decay

READING: READING COMPREHENSION

● Lesson 14: Fiction

Directions: Read the passage. Choose the best answer to each question. Fill in the circle for the answer of your choice.

Example

The sun beamed down on the sweltering city streets. Carl and Evan moped along, sweating.

"We've got to beat this heat," groaned Carl.

"Let's take the subway to the beach," suggested Evan.

"Neither of us has enough money for the fare," said Carl. "And we certainly can't afford an air-conditioned movie."

"I know," cried Evan, "let's go to Andrew's."

"Great idea," responded Carl. "He has air-conditioning and a pool!"

A. **What is the setting for this story?**

- Ⓐ a country road
- Ⓑ Carl's apartment
- Ⓒ a city street
- Ⓓ a small town

 Clue

Skim the passage so you have an understanding of what it is about. Then skim the questions. Answer the easiest questions first, and then look back to the passage to find the answers.

● Practice

Cyber Love

Alex sat next to the girl of his dreams every day in science, math, and computer applications. Every day CeCe smiled at Alex with her pretty, silver smile. Like Alex, she too wore braces. She wrote notes to him during class and laughed at all his jokes. Alex thought she liked him, but he was too shy to ask. He worried that the year would pass without ever learning for certain.

When Valentine's Day approached, Alex thought he had a chance. He would send her a special valentine. Unfortunately, he had no money. He was desperate, so desperate that he broke down and talked to his dad.

When Alex's dad said, "Try cyberspace," Alex was confused. He wondered how the Internet could help him. But when he visited the Free Virtual Valentine Web site, he knew his problem was solved. He chose a musical valentine and e-mailed it to CeCe at school.

GO ON

READING: READING COMPREHENSION

● **Lesson 14: Fiction (cont.)**

On Valentine's Day, Alex waited patiently for CeCe to open her e-mail. He tried to look busy as he watched her out of the corner of his eye. CeCe whispered, "You sent me a message," as she clicked on the hot link to Alex's valentine. Then she turned to Alex and said, "You're great."

I'm great, Alex thought to himself. *She likes me. If only I'd discovered cyberspace a long time ago.*

1. **Which sentence best summarizes the main idea of this story?**
    - (A) Alex liked school.
    - (B) Alex was very shy.
    - (C) Alex wanted to know if CeCe liked him.
    - (D) Cyberspace is a great way to show your love.

2. **Which detail from the story does not show that CeCe liked Alex?**
    - (F) She smiled at him.
    - (G) She laughed at his jokes.
    - (H) She sent him notes.
    - (J) She and Alex both wore braces.

3. **What can we conclude about CeCe from the first paragraph?**
    - (A) She had a good sense of humor.
    - (B) She was intelligent.
    - (C) She liked Alex.
    - (D) She liked Alex's braces.

4. **Why didn't Alex ask CeCe if she liked him?**
    - (F) He didn't think to ask.
    - (G) He was too shy.
    - (H) He didn't like girls.
    - (J) The year went by too quickly.

5. **What is the climax of this story?**
    - (A) Alex waits to see CeCe's response to his valentine.
    - (B) CeCe tells Alex that he is great.
    - (C) Alex talks to his dad.
    - (D) CeCe laughs at his jokes.

6. **What is the purpose of this story?**
    - (F) To illustrate how to combat shyness with girls
    - (G) To explain how Alex discovered that CeCe liked him
    - (H) To illustrate how to send a valentine through cyberspace
    - (J) To illustrate that it pays to ask parents for advice

READING: READING COMPREHENSION

● Lesson 15: Nonfiction

Directions: Read the passage. Choose the best answer to each question. Fill in the circle for the answer of your choice.

Example

The Trans-Canadian Highway is the first ocean-to-ocean highway in Canada and the longest paved road in the world. After twelve years of work, the 4,859-mile highway was completed in September 1962. This highway made it possible for a person to drive from coast to coast and remain within Canada for the entire trip.

A. This paragraph tells mainly —

- Ⓐ about highways in Canada
- Ⓑ why the Trans-Canadian Highway is helpful
- Ⓒ when the Trans-Canadian Highway was built
- Ⓓ the location of the longest road

 Clue

Skim the passage so you have an understanding of what it is about. Then skim the questions. Answer the easiest questions first, and then look back to the passage to find the answer.

● Practice

Imagine this. You wake up to discover that a fresh layer of glistening snow covers the ground. After breakfast, you pull on your cold weather gear and hop on your bike. For some, this thought is unimaginable. For others, this activity, called ice biking, is an enjoyable form of recreation or even a way to commute to work. Ice bikers race and even go on camping trips.

If you think ice biking sounds fun, it is easy to get started. Ice bikers suggest that starting is just as easy as not putting your bike away when the weather grows cold. Just continue riding your bike. They suggest that you begin by riding your bike one day at a time. Plus, don't be foolhardy. Dress appropriately and watch the wind chill.

1. **What is the best way to begin ice biking?**

- Ⓐ Go out and buy a new bike.
- Ⓑ Don't put your bike away when it gets cold.
- Ⓒ Ride just a few minutes each day.
- Ⓓ Watch the wind chill.

2. **Which describes an activity enjoyed by ice bikers?**

- Ⓕ commuting to work
- Ⓖ camping
- Ⓗ racing
- Ⓙ All of the above

 STOP

━━━━ *READING: READING COMPREHENSION* ━━━━

● Lesson 16: Nonfiction

Directions: Read the passage. Choose the best answer to each question. Fill in the circle for the answer of your choice.

Example

The liver is the largest of the body's glands. It helps the body absorb food by producing a fluid that breaks down the food taken into the body. The liver clears the blood of many harmful products it can absorb. The liver also stores sugar for future use and makes sure that the heart does not become overloaded with blood.

A. How many functions does the liver perform?

- (A) one
- (B) two
- (C) three
- (D) four

 Clue **Skim the passage and questions. Look back to the passage if you are unsure of the answers.**

● Practice

The Ship of the Desert

Nomads who crisscross the Sahara Desert of North Africa rely on a most unique animal for transportation—the dromedary, or one-humped camel. Because it is indispensable to desert travel, the dromedary is sometimes called the "ship of the desert."

Several factors make the dromedary suitable for long desert trips. It can go for long periods without nourishment. The hump on a camel's back serves as its food reserve. When it has little to eat, it converts the fat from its hump into energy. The camel's hump can weigh up to 80 pounds or more. When the animal has to rely on its reservoir of fat, the hump becomes much smaller. Thus, it is easy to recognize a well-fed camel by the size of its hump.

Many people believe that camels store water in their humps. This is not true. Their ability to go for days without drinking is due to other factors. First, camels are able to drink large quantities of water at one time. Some have been known to gulp 53 gallons in one day. Second, the camel sweats very little and can tolerate greater body temperatures. Consequently, it retains most of the water it drinks and can travel several hundred miles before replenishing its supply.

Other physical characteristics enable the camel to endure harsh desert conditions. It can completely close its nostrils, thus protecting it from the stinging effects of sandstorms. Its eyes are shielded from sand and sun by overhanging lids and long lashes, and its broad, padded feet keep it from sinking into the soft sand. No other animal is better equipped for life in the desert than the camel.

GO ON

READING: READING COMPREHENSION

● **Lesson 16: Nonfiction (cont.)**

1. **What is the main idea expressed in this story?**
   - (A) The dromedary is the ideal animal for desert life.
   - (B) The camel's hump serves as its food reservoir.
   - (C) The dromedary is called the "ship of the desert."
   - (D) Camels do not store water in their humps.

2. **Which characteristic does not help the camel to survive in the desert?**
   - (F) A camel can drink up to 53 gallons of water in one day.
   - (G) A camel can close its nostrils.
   - (H) A camel sweats very little.
   - (J) A camel is indispensable to desert travel.

3. **What cannot be concluded from reading this passage?**
   - (A) A camel can survive a long time without eating.
   - (B) A dromedary camel is easier to ride than a Bactrian camel.
   - (C) Camels have many features that equip them for cold weather.
   - (D) Both B and C

4. **Which of these statements is a fact?**
   - (F) Nomads prefer camels to all other pack animals.
   - (G) The Bactrian camel is the best camel for desert travel.
   - (H) A camel's broad, padded feet protect it from sinking in soft sand.
   - (J) Camels enjoy hot weather.

5. **Which additional detail would support the title of this story?**
   - (A) Nomads use camel's hair to weave cloth to make tents.
   - (B) Camels are strong animals capable of carrying loads up to a thousand pounds.
   - (C) Camel's milk and meat are often part of the nomad's diet.
   - (D) Camels can be stubborn.

6. **What is the author's purpose for this passage?**
   - (F) to entertain
   - (G) to inform
   - (H) to persuade
   - (J) to sell a product

STOP

READING: READING COMPREHENSION

● **Lesson 17: Nonfiction**

Directions: Read the passage. Choose the best answer to each question. Fill in the circle for the answer of your choice.

Example

Though Americans take pride in the accomplishments of the pony express, few people know of an earlier and equally remarkable postal service. Eight hundred years before the pony express operated, messages traveled 150 miles a day without the aid of a horse. Incan runners were spaced about three miles apart over a stone road that stretched 5,000 miles. These relay runners were the "express mail" carriers of their time.

A. The best nickname for these Incan messengers would be —

  (A) the pony express
  (B) the Incan express
  (C) the horseless carriage
  (D) the horseless express

Skim the passage and questions. Look back to the passage if you are unsure of the answers.

● **Practice**

The Man Behind the Faces

If you have never heard of Gutzon Borglum, you are not alone. Even though he was the sculptor responsible for the carvings on Mount Rushmore, many people do not know him by name.

Gutzon Borglum was born in Idaho in 1867 to Danish parents. He became interested in art early in life. He spent time studying in Paris then returned home to concentrate on sculpture. At the beginning of his career, Gutzon created many large sculptures, some which are quite famous. He also worked on the early stages of the carving of General Robert E. Lee at Stone Mountain, Virginia.

Gutzon was patriotic and outspoken. He lived during a time in American history called "the Colossal Age." This meant that big things were happening. For this reason, Gutzon Borglum became known as an artist who did things on a grand scale.

Borglum wanted to create a large monument to four American Presidents who brought our country into the modern age. He located Mount Rushmore, a 5,725-foot granite mountain

GO ON

READING: READING COMPREHENSION

● Lesson 17: Nonfiction (cont.)

in South Dakota and began his sculptures in 1927. Working on one at a time, Gutzon and his team carved the faces of George Washington, Thomas Jefferson, Abraham Lincoln, and Theodore Roosevelt into the mountainside.

Gutzon died in 1941, but his son, Lincoln, continued the work on Mount Rushmore. Today Mount Rushmore is one of the most-visited national monuments.

1. **What is this article mainly about?**
   - (A) the beginning of "the Colossal Age"
   - (B) Gutzon Borglum's life
   - (C) Borglum's great work, Mount Rushmore
   - (D) art on a grand scale

2. **According to the passage, Gutzon Borglum did things on a grand scale. What does doing something "on a grand scale" probably mean?**
   - (F) creating things with intricate designs
   - (G) making things that are very large and impressive
   - (H) doing things well and with great care
   - (J) doing things that take artistic talent

3. **Based on your answer for number 2, which of the following would you consider to be done on a grand scale?**
   - (A) a painting as tall as a house
   - (B) a painting of a large, royal family
   - (C) a drawing of the tallest building in the world
   - (D) a life-size sculpture of a man

4. **Which of these statements about Mount Rushmore is true according to information in the article?**
   - (F) Mount Rushmore is located in North Dakota.
   - (G) It is located in South Dakota.
   - (H) It is more famous than Stone Mountain.
   - (J) It is the largest mountain in the country.

5. **What detail does not support the idea of Gutzon as an artist?**
   - (A) Gutzon went to Paris to study art.
   - (B) He became interested in art early in his life.
   - (C) Gutzon was patriotic and outspoken.
   - (D) He created many large sculptures.

READING: READING COMPREHENSION
SAMPLE TEST

● **Directions:** Read the passage. Choose the best answer to each question. Fill in the circle for the answer of your choice.

Example

Penny arrived early at the Johnson's because it was her first time to sit for their little girl, Lori. Lori looked at Penny. Lori was very petite. Her blond hair was pulled back into two ponytails, and her bright smile made even her freckles sparkle. Lori asked Penny to play dolls with her.

E1. What can we know about Lori from reading the paragraph above?

- Ⓐ Lori is an intelligent little girl.
- Ⓑ Lori is a pretty little girl.
- Ⓒ Lori is a little girl with a bright smile.
- Ⓓ Penny will have no problems babysitting Lori.

By Saturday Noon

Saturday noon is one of those special times in our house. When I say special, I don't mean good special. By Saturday noon, my sisters and I need to have our bedrooms pristine.

When Dad inspects our rooms, he is like an army sergeant doing the white-glove test. If anything is out of place, if any clothes are left on the floor, and if your dresser isn't cleaned off and shiny, you don't get to go anywhere that day.

That isn't hard for Margaret. She's a neat freak. But Chelsea and I are normal, which is the problem—two normal sisters sharing a bedroom. On Monday, we start our separate piles: dirty clothes, wrinkled clothes, clothes we decided not to wear but forgot to hang up. By Wednesday, it's hard to find the floor. By Friday, the tops of the dressers are loaded. Plus, Mom won't let us throw everything down the laundry chute. "Sort it," she says.

Usually, we have enough time to get our clothes all folded and hung by noon, but last Saturday, Chelsea got sick. She spent the morning in the bathroom. I was left to clean the room alone. I had plans to shop with Jen.

At 10:00, Jen decided she wanted to leave early. I was desperate, so I shoved everything under Chelsea's bed, dusted the dressers, plumped the pillows, and called Dad for a room check.

Dad started his checklist. Everything was okay until Dad got to my closet. He turned and asked, "Where are all your clothes, Sara?"

"Dirty," I confessed.

Dad looked around until he spied the clothes under Chelsea's bed.

"Dirty?" he asked.

GO ON

I winced. "I must have missed those."

"Call Jen. You're not going shopping today," he said.

By Saturday noon, I was sick right alongside Chelsea. Mom said, "It's a good thing you didn't go shopping." I figured it was just the opposite. If I had gone shopping, I would never have gotten sick.

1. **The words in the title "Saturday Noon" are used three times in the story. Why is that time important to Sara?**

    (A) Chelsea wanted to go shopping.

    (B) It was the deadline for having her room clean, which determined whether or not she could go out that day.

    (C) It was the time Sara had to have the laundry done.

    (D) It was when she got sick.

2. **How is Margaret different from Sara and Chelsea?**

    (F) She is older.

    (G) She is younger.

    (H) She is very neat.

    (J) She always goes out on Saturdays.

3. **What does the word _pristine_ mean in this story?**

    (A) very clean

    (B) organized

    (C) packed

    (D) untidy

4. **Which of the following is not one of Sara's excuses for not getting her room clean?**

    (F) Sara's mom will not let her throw clothes down the laundry chute.

    (G) Chelsea got sick and couldn't help.

    (H) Jen wanted to leave early.

    (J) Her mom should clean her room.

5. **What is this story's plot?**

    (A) Sara can't wait to go shopping.

    (B) Sara knows she needs to have her room clean by Saturday noon, but blames everyone but herself for her room not being clean.

    (C) Sara allows her laundry to build up.

    (D) Sara's dad has unrealistic expectations for Sara.

6. **Which title below best fits this story?**

    (F) The Blame Game

    (G) Cleaning Is Not Normal

    (H) Shopping with Jen

    (J) Laundry Woes

GO ON

Name _____ Date_____

Read the passage. Choose the best answer to each question. Fill in the circle for the answer of your choice.

Example

When a baby kangaroo is born, it is as big as your thumb. The baby, called a joey, cannot see, hear, walk, or jump. It crawls into the pouch on its mother's stomach and remains there about eight months. During that time, its body grows and develops more fully.

E2. **What is the main idea of this paragraph?**
- Ⓕ Newborn joeys are small and defenseless.
- Ⓖ Newborn joeys are as small as your thumb.
- Ⓗ A mother kangaroo has it easy.
- Ⓙ Joeys are baby kangaroos.

Maternal Fish Father

In the warm and temperate waters of the world live two unusual fish: the sea horse and its relative, the pipefish.

The sea horse, so-called because its head resembles a horse, is a small fish about two to eight inches long. It swims by moving the dorsal fin on its back. It is the only fish with a prehensile tail that it uses, like a monkey, to coil around and cling to seaweed.

The pipefish is named for its long snout, which looks like a thin pipe. When its body is straight, the pipefish resembles a slender snake. Its body forms an S shape and is propelled by its rear fins.

But it is not appearance that makes the sea horse and pipefish unique. It is their paternal roles. With both fish, the female's responsibility ends when she lays and deposits her eggs. From that point on, the male takes over and, in a manner of speaking, gives birth to the babies.

Both the male sea horse and pipefish have pouchlike organs on their undersides in which the female deposits her eggs. Here the young fish stay and are nourished for either a few days or for several weeks, depending on the species. When the baby sea horses are ready to be born, the father sea horse attaches itself to a plant and actually goes through the pangs of childbirth. As the sea horse bends back and forth, the wall of its brood pouch contracts. With each spasm, a baby fish is introduced into the world of the sea. The birth of the baby pipefish is less dramatic. The father's pouch simply opens, and the offspring swim off on their own.

GO ON

Name _____ Date _____

READING: READING COMPREHENSION
SAMPLE TEST (cont.)

7. What is the main idea of this passage?

Ⓐ The pipefish and the sea horse fathers are unusual because of the way their offspring are born.

Ⓑ Sea horses resemble horses but have tales like monkeys.

Ⓒ Female pipefish and sea horses are lazy.

Ⓓ Sea horses make good pets.

8. Which statement does not describe a sea horse?

Ⓕ The sea horse's head resembles a horse.

Ⓖ The sea horse's body is propelled by a rear fin.

Ⓗ The sea horse uses its snout to cling to seaweed.

Ⓙ The sea horse has a prehensile tail.

9. Which statement seems to say that the role of the pipefish is less difficult than that of the seahorse?

Ⓐ The baby pipefish swim off.

Ⓑ The father's pouch simply opens.

Ⓒ The pipefish's body is shaped like an S.

Ⓓ The pipefish has a long, thin snout.

10. Which statement is an opinion?

Ⓕ Male sea horses and pipefish are very good fathers.

Ⓖ Sea horses are from two to eight inches long.

Ⓗ Sea horses move by the use of their dorsal fins.

Ⓙ The wall of the male sea horse's brood pouch contracts.

11. What is the author's purpose?

Ⓐ to compare and contrast two fish

Ⓑ to entertain

Ⓒ to persuade

Ⓓ to confuse

STOP

ANSWER SHEET

STUDENT'S NAME

LAST | **FIRST** | **MI**

(A–Z bubble columns for name)

SCHOOL

TEACHER

FEMALE ○   MALE ○

BIRTH DATE

MONTH	DAY		YEAR

MONTH: JAN ○ FEB ○ MAR ○ APR ○ MAY ○ JUN ○ JUL ○ AUG ○ SEP ○ OCT ○ NOV ○ DEC ○

DAY: (0,1,2,3) (0,1,2,3,4,5,6,7,8,9,0)

YEAR: (0,1,2,3,4,5,6,7,8,9)

GRADE
(5) (6) (7)

Part 1: VOCABULARY

E1	Ⓐ Ⓑ Ⓒ Ⓓ	6	Ⓕ Ⓖ Ⓗ Ⓙ	13	Ⓐ Ⓑ Ⓒ Ⓓ	20	Ⓕ Ⓖ Ⓗ Ⓙ	27	Ⓐ Ⓑ Ⓒ Ⓓ	34	Ⓕ Ⓖ Ⓗ Ⓙ
E2	Ⓕ Ⓖ Ⓗ Ⓙ	7	Ⓐ Ⓑ Ⓒ Ⓓ	14	Ⓕ Ⓖ Ⓗ Ⓙ	21	Ⓐ Ⓑ Ⓒ Ⓓ	28	Ⓕ Ⓖ Ⓗ Ⓙ	35	Ⓐ Ⓑ Ⓒ Ⓓ
1	Ⓐ Ⓑ Ⓒ Ⓓ	8	Ⓕ Ⓖ Ⓗ Ⓙ	15	Ⓐ Ⓑ Ⓒ Ⓓ	22	Ⓕ Ⓖ Ⓗ Ⓙ	29	Ⓐ Ⓑ Ⓒ Ⓓ		
2	Ⓕ Ⓖ Ⓗ Ⓙ	9	Ⓐ Ⓑ Ⓒ Ⓓ	16	Ⓕ Ⓖ Ⓗ Ⓙ	23	Ⓐ Ⓑ Ⓒ Ⓓ	30	Ⓕ Ⓖ Ⓗ Ⓙ		
3	Ⓐ Ⓑ Ⓒ Ⓓ	10	Ⓕ Ⓖ Ⓗ Ⓙ	17	Ⓐ Ⓑ Ⓒ Ⓓ	24	Ⓕ Ⓖ Ⓗ Ⓙ	31	Ⓐ Ⓑ Ⓒ Ⓓ		
4	Ⓕ Ⓖ Ⓗ Ⓙ	11	Ⓐ Ⓑ Ⓒ Ⓓ	18	Ⓕ Ⓖ Ⓗ Ⓙ	25	Ⓐ Ⓑ Ⓒ Ⓓ	32	Ⓕ Ⓖ Ⓗ Ⓙ		
5	Ⓐ Ⓑ Ⓒ Ⓓ	12	Ⓕ Ⓖ Ⓗ Ⓙ	19	Ⓐ Ⓑ Ⓒ Ⓓ	26	Ⓕ Ⓖ Ⓗ Ⓙ	33	Ⓐ Ⓑ Ⓒ Ⓓ		

Part 2: READING COMPREHENSION

E1	Ⓐ Ⓑ Ⓒ Ⓓ	7	Ⓐ Ⓑ Ⓒ Ⓓ	14	Ⓕ Ⓖ Ⓗ Ⓙ	21	Ⓐ Ⓑ Ⓒ Ⓓ	28	Ⓕ Ⓖ Ⓗ Ⓙ
1	Ⓐ Ⓑ Ⓒ Ⓓ	8	Ⓕ Ⓖ Ⓗ Ⓙ	15	Ⓐ Ⓑ Ⓒ Ⓓ	22	Ⓕ Ⓖ Ⓗ Ⓙ	29	Ⓐ Ⓑ Ⓒ Ⓓ
2	Ⓕ Ⓖ Ⓗ Ⓙ	9	Ⓐ Ⓑ Ⓒ Ⓓ	16	Ⓕ Ⓖ Ⓗ Ⓙ	23	Ⓐ Ⓑ Ⓒ Ⓓ		
3	Ⓐ Ⓑ Ⓒ Ⓓ	10	Ⓕ Ⓖ Ⓗ Ⓙ	17	Ⓐ Ⓑ Ⓒ Ⓓ	24	Ⓕ Ⓖ Ⓗ Ⓙ		
4	Ⓕ Ⓖ Ⓗ Ⓙ	11	Ⓐ Ⓑ Ⓒ Ⓓ	18	Ⓕ Ⓖ Ⓗ Ⓙ	25	Ⓐ Ⓑ Ⓒ Ⓓ		
5	Ⓐ Ⓑ Ⓒ Ⓓ	12	Ⓕ Ⓖ Ⓗ Ⓙ	19	Ⓐ Ⓑ Ⓒ Ⓓ	26	Ⓕ Ⓖ Ⓗ Ⓙ		
6	Ⓕ Ⓖ Ⓗ Ⓙ	13	Ⓐ Ⓑ Ⓒ Ⓓ	20	Ⓕ Ⓖ Ⓗ Ⓙ	27	Ⓐ Ⓑ Ⓒ Ⓓ		

Name _____ Date_____

READING PRACTICE TEST

● **Part 1: Vocabulary**

Directions: For item E1, find the word that means the same or almost the same as the underlined word. For item E2, fill in the circle for the answer you think is correct. Then follow the directions for each part of this test.

Examples

E1. <u>artificial</u> diamond
- (A) fake
- (B) genuine
- (C) exquisite
- (D) authentic

E2. Which of these words probably comes from the Latin word *familiaris*, which means "domestic"?
- (F) farmer
- (G) familiar
- (H) famous
- (J) domicile

For numbers 1–13, find the word or words that mean the same or almost the same as the underlined word.

1. surprising <u>outcome</u>
   - (A) relationship
   - (B) appointment
   - (C) result
   - (D) announcement

2. <u>hideous</u> mask
   - (F) lovely
   - (G) funny
   - (H) monstrous
   - (J) false

3. <u>audible</u> sigh
   - (A) heard
   - (B) silent
   - (C) austere
   - (D) angry

4. <u>desolate</u> landscape
   - (F) forested
   - (G) barren
   - (H) desirable
   - (J) unnatural

5. To <u>subside</u> is to —
   - (A) continue
   - (B) grow louder
   - (C) cease
   - (D) be intermittent

6. A <u>cunning</u> plan is —
   - (F) clever
   - (G) unoriginal
   - (H) original
   - (J) detailed

7. A <u>monotone</u> speech is —
   - (A) exciting
   - (B) lively
   - (C) dull
   - (D) hesitant

8. To <u>assert</u> is to —
   - (F) declare
   - (G) argue
   - (H) proceed
   - (J) boast

GO ON

READING PRACTICE TEST
Part 1: Vocabulary (cont.)

9. **The old woman was very frail.**
   Frail means —
   - (A) hardy
   - (B) determined
   - (C) delicate
   - (D) forgetful

10. **Daphne's excuse was legitimate.**
    Legitimate means the same as —
    - (F) false
    - (G) honest
    - (H) faulty
    - (J) incredible

11. **Aaron Baron was very illustrious.**
    Illustrious means —
    - (A) famous
    - (B) infamous
    - (C) intelligent
    - (D) sickly

12. **Juanita's complexion was wan.**
    Wan means —
    - (F) tan
    - (G) ashen
    - (H) bright
    - (J) swarthy

13. **The crowd jostled Justin.**
    Jostled means —
    - (A) ridiculed
    - (B) honored
    - (C) pushed
    - (D) ignored

For numbers 14–19, choose the word that means the opposite of the underlined word.

14. **a gleeful response**
    - (F) joyous
    - (G) gloomy
    - (H) cheerful
    - (J) reluctant

15. **absurd situation**
    - (A) ridiculous
    - (B) sensible
    - (C) unbelievable
    - (D) embarrassing

16. **arid climate**
    - (F) dry
    - (G) airy
    - (H) fertile
    - (J) barren

17. **animated conversation**
    - (A) lively
    - (B) dull
    - (C) energetic
    - (D) one-sided

18. **sodden clothing**
    - (F) soaked
    - (G) spongy
    - (H) dry
    - (J) filthy

19. **essential ingredient**
    - (A) necessary
    - (B) unnecessary
    - (C) important
    - (D) additional

GO ON

READING PRACTICE TEST
Part 1: Vocabulary (cont.)

For numbers 20–23, choose the word that correctly completes both sentences.

20. He discovered an underground _____.

    Rachel read the _____ several times.

    (F) book
    (G) passage
    (H) civilization
    (J) letter

21. Michael's arm was in a _____.

    Chondra was part of the _____.

    (A) sleeve
    (B) crew
    (C) cast
    (D) mold

22. Akiko had a _____ in her brow.

    The farmer made a _____ with his plow.

    (F) furrow
    (G) wrinkle
    (H) trench
    (J) scar

23. Sara's hair was _____.

    Matthew's friend _____ at him.

    (A) scowled
    (B) wild
    (C) tangled
    (D) snarled

24. Will the children spruce up their rooms?

    In which sentence does the word spruce mean the same thing as in the sentence above?

    (F) They planted a spruce.
    (G) We used spruce to build our house.
    (H) The volunteers will spruce up the playground.
    (J) Maggie climbed up the spruce.

25. Andre bounced the ball.

    In which sentence does the word bounced mean the same thing as in the sentence above?

    (A) Kate bounced back after her surgery.
    (B) Mrs. Smith's check bounced.
    (C) The Ping-Pong ball bounced off the table.
    (D) The kangaroo bounced across the field.

For numbers 26 and 27, choose the answer that best defines the underlined part.

26. prepare   preoccupy
    (F) after
    (G) before
    (H) because of
    (J) over

27. patience   obedience
    (A) state or condition of being
    (B) full of
    (C) having, tending to
    (D) without

GO ON

READING PRACTICE TEST
Part 1: Vocabulary (cont.)

28. Which of these words probably comes from the Latin word *gratia* meaning "grace"?

- (F) grade
- (G) grasp
- (H) gracious
- (J) regret

29. Inhale is to exhale as tense is to —

- (A) breathe
- (B) relax
- (C) nervous
- (D) gasp

30. Her favorite _____ was "Better safe than sorry."

Which of these words means "saying"?

- (F) craving
- (G) bias
- (H) maxim
- (J) gild

31. The man _____ an oak.

Which of these words means "to cut down with an ax"?

- (A) hewed
- (B) heaved
- (C) haunch
- (D) sliced

Read the paragraph. Choose the word below the paragraph that fits best in each numbered blank.

In October 1985, a whale caused quite a _____ (32) near the _____ (33) of California. The whale, a _____ (34) so large that its home is the Pacific Ocean, swam under the Golden Gate Bridge and up the Sacramento River. After more than three weeks, the whale finally reversed its _____ (35) and headed back toward the ocean.

32.
- (F) collision
- (G) stir
- (H) boycott
- (J) meddle

33.
- (A) city
- (B) island
- (C) coast
- (D) coax

34.
- (F) fish
- (G) amphibian
- (H) plebeian
- (J) creature

35.
- (A) bow
- (B) course
- (C) ballasts
- (D) opinion

STOP

READING PRACTICE TEST

● Part 2: Reading Comprehension

Directions: Read the passage. Choose the best answer to each question. Fill in the circle for the answer of your choice.

Example

Jade begged her father to let her get a cat, but he worried that she wouldn't take care of it. So Jade worked hard to show how responsible she was. She even took out the trash every week and did all her homework every day after she got home from school.

When Jade's birthday came, she received a board game and some new clothes. Then, at the last minute, her father handed her a shoebox—something was squirming inside!

E1. What do you think will happen next?

Ⓐ Jade will open the box to find a puppy.

Ⓑ Jade will open the box to discover a kitten.

Ⓒ Jade will open the box to find her little brother.

Ⓓ Jade will not open the box.

Read this passage about a boy who discovers two coins. Then answer the questions on the next page.

One Afternoon in March

One afternoon in March, I found two silver dollars shining in a half-melted snow bank. I instantly thought of buried treasure. So I dug through the snow searching for more. All I ended up with were two really cold hands. I slipped the two coins in my pocket and went home colder but richer.

The next morning, Megan and her little sister were searching the snow banks. *Finders keepers* was my first thought. I didn't need to get to the *losers weepers* part since Moira was already crying for real.

"I dropped them right here," she said between tears. Her hands were red from digging in the snow.

"Maybe they got shoved down the street by the snow plow. Let's try over there," Megan said optimistically.

They'll never know was my second thought, as I walked past them toward Tyler's house.

"Phil, have you seen two silver dollars?" Megan called. Moira looked up from the snow bank with hope bright in her eyes.

"Coins?" *Look innocent* was my third thought.

GO ON ⟩

READING PRACTICE TEST
Part 2: Reading Comprehension (cont.)

"Yes, Moira dropped two silver dollars somewhere around here yesterday."

"Yeah," said Moira, "they're big and heavy." She brushed her red hands off on her jacket and wiped the tears from her eyes. Her eyes were as red as her hands.

Lie, I thought, but said, "As a matter of fact," I hesitated, "I dug two coins out of that snow bank yesterday. I wondered who might have lost them."

Moira ran to me and gave me a bear hug. "Oh, thank you, thank you!"

I couldn't help but smile.

---

1. **What is the main idea of this story?**

   Ⓐ It is okay to lie if you think you will get away with it.

   Ⓑ It is always better to be honest than rich.

   Ⓒ "Finders keepers, losers weepers" is not a good saying to live by.

   Ⓓ Both B and C apply.

2. **How did Phil probably feel at the end of the story? He felt —**

   Ⓕ angry with himself for being honest.

   Ⓖ angry with Megan and Moira.

   Ⓗ hopeful that he would find another buried treasure.

   Ⓙ disappointed at having to give up the coins but glad that he had been honest.

3. **What is the problem in this story?**

   Ⓐ Moira has lost two silver dollars in the snow.

   Ⓑ Phil does not want to give up the coins he found.

   Ⓒ Phil does not want to help Moira find her coins.

   Ⓓ Megan does not want to help her sister.

4. **Which statement below is a fact?**

   Ⓕ Phil thinks only of his own wants.

   Ⓖ Moira cries a lot.

   Ⓗ Moira and Phil should be wearing mittens when out in the snow.

   Ⓙ Moira is crying because she has lost her silver dollars.

5. **What is the setting of this story?**

   Ⓐ outside on a March day

   Ⓑ outside on a warm, summer day

   Ⓒ a cold, winter day

   Ⓓ the view outside a window

6. **What would be a good title for this story?**

   Ⓕ Frostbitten Fingers

   Ⓖ Finders Keepers, Losers Weepers

   Ⓗ A Fistful of Dollars

   Ⓙ Honesty Is Best

GO ON

Name _____ Date _____

Read this story about a Native American girl. Then answer the questions on the next page.

A New Tipi

Fingers of frost tickled at Little Deer's feet. It was a chilly fall morning, but there was no time for Little Deer to snuggle beneath her buffalo skins. It was going to be a busy day, helping her mother to finish the cover for their family's new tipi.

Little Deer slid her tunic over her head and fastened her moccasins. Wrapping herself up in another skin, she walked outside to survey the work they had done so far. The tipi cover was beautiful and nearly complete. The vast semicircle was spread across the ground, a patchwork in various shades of brown. After her father and brothers had killed the buffalo, she and her mother had carefully cured and prepared the skins, stretching them and scraping them until they were buttery soft. Then with needles made from bone and thread made from animal sinew, they had carefully sewn the hides together until they formed a huge canvas nearly thirty feet across.

After they finished the cover today, it would be ready to mount on the lodge poles. Little Deer's father had traded with another tribe for fourteen tall, wooden poles. They would stack the poles together in a cone shape, lashing them together with more rope made from animal sinews.

Then they would carefully stretch the cover over the poles, forming a snug, watertight home. Little Deer smiled in anticipation. She could just imagine the cozy glow of the fire through the tipi walls at night.

READING PRACTICE TEST
Part 2: Reading Comprehension (cont.)

7. **What is this story mainly about?**

   (A) hunting

   (B) building a tipi

   (C) the uses of buffalo

   (D) the life of a Native American girl

8. **Which sentence below is not a step in the process of making a tipi?**

   (F) Stretch the cover over the poles.

   (G) Cure and prepare the skins.

   (H) Sew the hides together.

   (J) Make clothing from the remaining pieces of hide.

9. **How does Little Deer feel about finishing the tipi?**

   (A) depressed

   (B) angry

   (C) excited

   (D) cold

10. **Which of these statements shows personification?**

    (F) Little Deer smiled in anticipation.

    (G) Little Deer slid her tunic over her head and fastened her moccasins.

    (H) The tipi cover was beautiful and nearly complete.

    (J) Fingers of frost tickled at Little Deer's feet.

11. **Where would this passage most likely be found?**

    (A) a historical novel

    (B) an encyclopedia

    (C) a science fiction story

    (D) a diary

12. **Which characteristic most accurately describes Little Deer?**

    (F) lazy

    (G) hardworking

    (H) clever

    (J) intelligent

GO ON

Read this story about a new girl at school. Then answer the questions on the next page.

A Handful of Pretty Flowers

When Shanda first arrived at school, she discovered to her dismay that a freckle-faced boy in her sixth-grade class was smitten with her. Because Shanda's family was new to the city, Shanda had not yet made any friends. She didn't feel comfortable asking the other students the boy's name. And he didn't offer his name, just a handful of pretty flowers.

Shanda soon learned the redheaded boy's name, Tommy. Whenever the class lined up for assembly or gym, he always smiled a crooked smile in her direction. Shanda felt uncomfortable with the attention he gave her, small though it was. Why did he like her anyway? On several occasions, Shanda tried to start a conversation with Tommy. But he always blushed, put his hands in his pockets, and looked down in embarrassment.

Gradually, Shanda developed a circle of friends. She finally felt happy in her new school. The only thing that still made her uncomfortable was Tommy with his crooked, shy smiles.

One day, as Shanda was walking down the hallway, Tommy came up alongside her. "Do you like animals?" he asked. Shanda was shocked. He had actually spoken to her.

Shanda turned to him and replied, "Hi, Tommy. Yeah, I like animals. We have lots of pets at my house. How about you?"

Shanda noticed how nervous Tommy had become as she talked. He even appeared to stop breathing for a moment. He whispered something about a dog and then hurried away. Shanda wondered if she had hurt his feelings by calling him Tommy. Maybe he liked to be called Tom.

A week later, Tommy reverently handed Shanda a photo. It was a snapshot of a beautiful collie. She had intelligent eyes and almost seemed to be smiling. Her ears were alert, and her face tilted questioningly. Shanda knew this was an important moment for Tommy. "What's her name?" she asked softly.

"Sh-, sh-, she was Shanda . . . like you. We had her since I was in kindergarten. Sh-, she's gone now."

READING PRACTICE TEST
Part 2: Reading Comprehension (cont.)

13. **What is this story mainly about?**

   (A) a girl has a hard time fitting in at a new school

   (B) a boy's love for his dog

   (C) a shy boy

   (D) a new girl at school and the shy boy who likes her

14. **In this story, what does the word *smitten* mean?**

   (F) struck by

   (G) attacked by

   (H) attracted to

   (J) bothered by

15. **From reading this story, we can conclude that —**

   (A) Tommy's dog has died, and he misses her.

   (B) Tommy's family now has a cat.

   (C) Tommy likes the name Shanda.

   (D) Tommy thinks Shanda is cute.

16. **What probably caused Tommy to give Shanda flowers?**

   (F) He felt sorry for her because she was a new girl.

   (G) She and his dog shared the name Shanda.

   (H) She had hair the same color as his collie.

   (J) She liked animals as much as he did.

17. **From whose point of view is this story told?**

   (A) Tommy's

   (B) Shanda's

   (C) the teacher's

   (D) Shanda's friend

18. **Which statement best describes Shanda?**

   (F) Shanda is popular.

   (G) Shanda likes Tommy.

   (H) Shanda shows kindness by asking about Tommy's dog.

   (J) Shanda is shy.

GO ON

Name _____ Date_____

Read this article about early radio. Then answer the questions on the next page.

Hi-Yo, Silver!

What did people do for entertainment before television? Today, the average child spends more time watching television than reading. Television is so much a part of daily life that many people cannot imagine what life was like before it.

Before television, there was radio. Radio was invented around 1916 from the telegraph. At first, it was used to get information quickly from one part of the country to another. By 1926, radios were common in homes. People listened to music, news, and shows in the same way we watch TV today. Television was not invented until the 1940s, and it did not gain popularity in homes until 1955.

Families gathered around their radios to listen to shows broadcast all over the world. One of the most popular radio shows was *The Lone Ranger*. This show was about a Texas Ranger and a faithful Native American, named Tonto, who tirelessly worked to stop evil. The Lone Ranger rode a white horse named Silver and wore a black mask. The Lone Ranger hid his identity, because he had been left for dead by a gang that ambushed and killed five other Texas Rangers. He vowed to find these desperadoes. His white hat, white horse, black mask, and his famous call, "Hi-yo, Silver. Away!" became symbols of the American Wild West hero.

Other famous radio heroes were the Shadow and the Green Hornet. Eventually, radio shows became famous television shows as well. Comedians and vaudeville stars made the transition from the stage to radio to television. Comedians such as Jack Benny, Red Skeleton, and George Burns had radio shows that became television favorites.

GO ON

READING PRACTICE TEST
Part 2: Reading Comprehension (cont.)

19. **What title best gives the main idea of this passage?**

    (A) The Lone Ranger Rides Again

    (B) Before Television Came Radio

    (C) Radio Stars Hit It Big on TV

    (D) The History of Radio

20. **What is not true of the passage?**

    (F) It gives a brief history of radio.

    (G) It tells about the transition from radio to television.

    (H) It focuses on *The Lone Ranger* show.

    (J) It shows how radio was far more popular than television.

21. **Which sentence below is an opinion?**

    (A) *The Lone Ranger* was the best radio show ever.

    (B) The Lone Ranger wore a white hat and black mask.

    (C) Tonto was the Lone Ranger's faithful companion.

    (D) *The Lone Ranger* took place in the American West.

22. **Which statement is true?**

    (F) Tonto rode a white horse named Silver.

    (G) Radio was invented in 1926.

    (H) Several radio shows later became popular TV shows.

    (J) Radio stars could not make it as television stars.

23. **Why do you suppose that *The Lone Ranger* was such a popular radio show?**

    (A) Families had nothing better to do with their free time.

    (B) It had the classic good guy against bad guys theme.

    (C) People liked the special effects.

    (D) People liked to watch the Lone Ranger and Tonto catch the bad guys.

GO ON

Name _____ Date_____

Read this article about humankind's quest for flight. Then answer the questions on the next page.

From Dreams to Reality

People have probably always dreamed of flight. As they watched birds fly, they wished that they could soar into the blue sky. As they watched the night sky, they wished they could explore the distant bright specks called stars. These dreams led inventors and scientists to risk their lives to achieve flight.

Orville and Wilbur Wright's first flight at Kitty Hawk in 1903 was only the beginning. Flight continued to improve and dreams soared further into space. The first manned space flight occurred in 1961 when Russian cosmonaut Yuri A. Gagarin orbited Earth a single time. In 1963, the first woman cosmonaut, Valentina Tereshkova, orbited Earth 48 times.

The Russians led the race for many years. In 1965, another cosmonaut, Alesksei A. Leonov, took the first space walk. In 1968, the Russians launched an unmanned spacecraft that orbited the moon. The pictures that returned to Earth encouraged man to take the next step to land on the moon.

The United States became the leader in the space race when *Apollo 11* landed on the moon in 1969. Neil Armstrong was the first man to step on the lunar surface. As he did so, he said these famous words, "That's one small step for a man, one giant leap for mankind." Later in 1969, Charles Conrad, Jr., and Alan L. Bean returned to the moon. In 1972, the United States completed its last mission to the moon, *Apollo 17*.

Today people continue their quest for space, gathering data from the *Mir* Space Station, which was launched in 1986. In addition, unmanned probes have flown deep into space toward the planets, sending back pictures and scientific readings.

READING PRACTICE TEST
Part 2: Reading Comprehension (cont.)

24. What is this passage mainly about?

- (F) famous cosmonauts
- (G) a brief history of human flight
- (H) the first flight
- (J) the space race

25. What happened first?

- (A) The *Mir* Space Station was launched.
- (B) Yuri Gagarin orbited Earth a single time.
- (C) Neil Armstrong walked on the moon.
- (D) The first woman orbited Earth.

26. Why do you suppose the race to achieve firsts in space travel was so important?

- (F) It prompted the United States to excel.
- (G) It encouraged cooperation between the two countries.
- (H) It discouraged people from being interested in space travel.
- (J) It developed fierce rivalry that led to many mistakes.

27. Which of these is an opinion?

- (A) The United States became the leader in the space race with the first landing on the moon.
- (B) All people have dreamed about being able to fly.
- (C) Today unmanned space probes explore space.
- (D) The Russians led the space race for several years.

28. What is the purpose of this passage?

- (F) to inform
- (G) to advertise
- (H) to entertain
- (J) to promote an idea

29. Which statement is false?

- (A) The first woman in space was Valentina Tereshkova.
- (B) The first landing on the moon was in 1969.
- (C) Russia achieved the first manned space flight.
- (D) The last landing on the moon in 1972 ended the space race.

Name _____ Date_____

LANGUAGE: LANGUAGE MECHANICS

● **Lesson 1: Punctuation**

Directions: Fill in the circle for the punctuation mark that is needed in the sentence. Fill in the circle for "None" if no more punctuation marks are needed.

Examples

A. Did you remember to brush your teeth

- Ⓐ .
- Ⓑ ?
- Ⓒ !
- Ⓓ None

B. "Keep up the good work," said Mrs. Goodwin.

- Ⓕ ,
- Ⓖ "
- Ⓗ .
- Ⓙ None

 Clue Look carefully at all the answer choices before you choose the one you think is correct. The missing punctuation mark may be at the end of the sentence or within it. Remember to look in both places.

● **Practice**

1. The yellow daffodils are very pretty
   - Ⓐ ,
   - Ⓑ .
   - Ⓒ ?
   - Ⓓ None

2. The robin, our state bird, lays blue eggs.
   - Ⓕ ;
   - Ⓖ !
   - Ⓗ .
   - Ⓙ None

3. "Stop, she called.
   - Ⓐ "
   - Ⓑ .
   - Ⓒ "
   - Ⓓ None

4. We visited Michigan Ohio, and Illinois.
   - Ⓕ .
   - Ⓖ ,
   - Ⓗ ;
   - Ⓙ None

5. "Hurry! School starts in ten minutes" said Isabel.
   - Ⓐ .
   - Ⓑ ?
   - Ⓒ ,
   - Ⓓ None

6. My favorite book *A Wrinkle in Time*, was already checked out.
   - Ⓕ .
   - Ⓖ :
   - Ⓗ ,
   - Ⓙ None

 GO ON

LANGUAGE: LANGUAGE MECHANICS

● Lesson 1: Punctuation (cont.)

For numbers 7–12, read each answer. Fill in the circle for the choice that has a punctuation error. If there are no mistakes, fill in the fourth circle.

7.
- (A) Our teacher Ms. Matthews, is
- (B) treating the class to ice cream sundaes
- (C) at Dairy Delight, my favorite ice cream shop.
- (D) No mistakes.

8.
- (F) Do you think you will complete
- (G) your report by Saturday.
- (H) I want to go to the beach on Sunday afternoon.
- (J) No mistakes.

9.
- (A) "I miss Grandpa," said Casey,
- (B) "Can we see him again soon?"
- (C) She loved her grandpa very much.
- (D) No mistakes.

10.
- (F) 8789 Rachel Dr.
- (G) Aarontown, MI 49543
- (H) May 22 2002.
- (J) No mistakes.

11.
- (A) Dear Melvin
- (B) I was so pleased to hear you won the
- (C) scholarship to computer camp. Good job!
- (D) No mistakes.

12.
- (F) You will have to show me all you learned?
- (G) Sincerely,
- (H) Margie
- (J) No mistakes.

For numbers 13–16, read each sentence. Choose the word or words that fit best in the blank and show the correct punctuation.

13. _____ please remember to wash your hands.
- (A) Brewster
- (B) Brewster:
- (C) Brewster,
- (D) "Brewster"

14. The _____ bite was bigger than its bark.
- (F) dogs
- (G) dog's
- (H) dogs's
- (J) dogs'

15. Charlene needed to bring _____ to the picnic.
- (A) plates, napkins, and cups
- (B) plates napkins and cups
- (C) plates, napkins, and cups,
- (D) plates, napkins and, cups

16. This bus is _____ we'll have to catch the next one.
- (F) full
- (G) full,
- (H) full;
- (J) full:

STOP

Name _____   Date_____

● **Lesson 2: Capitalization and Punctuation**

Directions: Fill in the circle for the answer that shows correct capitalization and punctuation.
Fill in the space for "Correct as it is" if the underlined part is correct.

Examples

A.
- (A) Yes you can go to the store.
- (B) No, you are not going to the mall.
- (C) Yes; i will help you
- (D) No: you may not have an iguana.

B. Raul, raise your <u>hand, please.</u>
- (F) hand please
- (G) hand, please?
- (H) hand please."
- (J) Correct as it is

 Clue Remember, you are looking for the answer that shows correct capitalization and punctuation. If you are not sure which answer is correct, take your best guess.

● **Practice**

1.
- (A) I have a new baby sister Nicole.
- (B) When did you see Ken.
- (C) His chinese water dragon eats crickets.
- (D) Chantell, would you like to go to the zoo with me?

2.
- (F) They have two weeks of school left but we have only one.
- (G) I want to go to Denver colorado to ski.
- (H) Ian and I went to the Detroit Zoo.
- (J) Lets take a trip to Chicago, Illinois.

3.
- (A) "Where would you like to go," asked the tour guide.
- (B) Mary's little sister said "She wanted to go home now."
- (C) "Can I stay overnight with Maria?" asked Sophie.
- (D) "I would love to visit new york, said Robert."

4. Austin likes the new <u>school but he</u> keeps getting lost.
- (F) school; but
- (G) school. But
- (H) school, but
- (J) Correct as it is

5. "Your hamster is <u>cool called</u> Mike.
- (A) cool, called
- (B) cool," called
- (C) cool?" called
- (D) Correct as it is

6. Cheryl hopes she has <u>Miss Phan's</u> class next year.
- (F) Miss Phans'
- (G) miss Phans
- (H) Miss Phans
- (J) Correct as it is

 GO ON

● Lesson 2: Capitalization and Punctuation (cont.)

Have you ever made homemade <u>clay.</u>
<u>these</u> **(7)** directions will help you create a
small quantity of clay. Take one cup of warm
<u>water one</u> **(8)** cup of salt, and two cups of
flour. Mix the ingredients together. Squeeze
the mixture until it is <u>smooth and</u> **(9)** does not
stick to your fingers. <u>Its ready</u> **(10)** for
modeling. You may also want to add food
coloring.

October 2, 2002

Marble Comix
2656 N. Way Blvd.
<u>Characterville, Ca, 12592</u> **(11)**

<u>Dear mr bulk</u> **(12)**
Please tell me how you were able to
turn green when you transformed. <u>My</u>
<u>friend robin</u> **(13)** really wants to know.
<u>Thanks I think you are cool?</u> **(14)**

Sincerely,

Bryce Payne

7.
   (A) clay, these
   (B) clay? These
   (C) clay; these
   (D) Correct as it is

8.
   (F) water: one
   (G) water one,
   (H) water, one
   (J) Correct as it is

9.
   (A) smooth, and
   (B) smooth. And
   (C) smooth; and
   (D) Correct as it is

10.
   (F) It's ready
   (G) Its' ready
   (H) It's ready,
   (J) Correct as it is

11.
   (A) Characterville, Ca 12592
   (B) Characterville, CA 12592
   (C) Characterville CA, 12592
   (D) Correct as it is

12.
   (F) Dear Mr Bulk,
   (G) Dear Mr. Bulk;
   (H) Dear Mr. Bulk,
   (J) Correct as it is

13.
   (A) My friend, Robin,
   (B) My, Friend Robin,
   (C) My friend Robin
   (D) Correct as it is

14.
   (F) Thanks; I think you are cool.
   (G) Thanks. I think you are cool.
   (H) Thanks. I think you are cool?
   (J) Correct as it is

GO ON

LANGUAGE: LANGUAGE MECHANICS

● **Lesson 2: Capitalization and Punctuation (cont.)**

For numbers 15 and 16, read the sentence. Fill in the circle for the choice that fits best in the blank and has correct capitalization and punctuation.

15. _____ invented a new laborsaving device.

   (A) Prof. Magee
   (B) Prof Magee
   (C) Prof. Magee,
   (D) Prof Magee,

16. **My parents are going to an island in the _____ us.**

   (F) Pacific ocean without
   (G) Pacific, Ocean without
   (H) pacific ocean, without
   (J) Pacific Ocean without

Read about one girl's unusual collection. Use the story to do numbers 17–20.

   (1) Some of my buttons are worth money, but most are just valuable to me. **(2)** I like to look at them because they remind me of people I know or things I have done. **(3)** My favorite buttons are the ones with jokes or funny pictures. **(4)** One of these is pink and says Im not just another pretty face, you know!" **(5)** Others have cartoon characters or animals on them. **(6)** When I visit a zoo or we go on vacation mom lets me buy a button. **(7)** She gives me a button every year on my birthday too. **(8)** Last year, my cousin barb sent me a button from Tucson Arizona?

17. **In sentence 4, says Im is best written —**

   (A) says I'm
   (B) says, "I'm
   (C) says "I'm
   (D) As it is

18. **In sentence 6, vacation mom lets is best written —**

   (F) vacation mom let's
   (G) vacation, mom lets
   (H) vacation, Mom lets
   (J) As it is

19. **In sentence 8, my cousin barb is best written —**

   (A) my cousin Barb
   (B) my cousin Barb,
   (C) my Cousin Barb,
   (D) As it is

20. **In sentence 8, Tucson Arizona? is best written —**

   (F) Tucson Arizona?
   (G) Tucson, Arizona.
   (H) Tucson, Arizona?
   (J) As it is

STOP

Name _____ Date _____

● **Directions:** For E1 and numbers 1–4, fill in the correct circle for the punctuation mark that is needed in the sentence. If no punctuation is needed, fill in the answer choice for "None."

Example

E1. **Where do you keep your cookies**

- (A) .
- (B) ?
- (C) !
- (D) None

---

1. **"That was great" exclaimed Stephen.**
   - (A) !
   - (B) .
   - (C) ,
   - (D) None

2. **We have band on Monday Wednesday, and Friday.**
   - (F) ;
   - (G) ,
   - (H) :
   - (J) None

3. **He said he wanted to go home now.**
   - (A) ,
   - (B) :
   - (C) "
   - (D) None

4. **"When can we leave? Nate inquired.**
   - (F) ,
   - (G) "
   - (H) :
   - (J) None

For numbers 5–7, read each answer. Fill in the circle for the choice that contains a punctuation error. If there is no mistake, fill in the fourth answer choice.

5. (A) "Karen, lets go to the haunted house
   (B) next weekend," said Deanna.

   (C) "That would be great," agreed Karen.
   (D) No mistakes

6. (F) Which one is it.
   (G) I can't tell
   (H) the difference between the two.
   (J) No mistakes

7. (A) Whose son is he?
   (B) I dont know him.
   (C) Does anyone recognize him?
   (D) No mistakes

For numbers 8 and 9, read the sentence. Choose the word or words that fit best in the blank and show the correct punctuation.

8. **Her list included the _____ clean room, do dishes, feed dog.**
   - (F) following,
   - (G) following:
   - (H) following;
   - (J) following

9. **The _____ we took at the zoo did not turn out.**
   - (A) pictures
   - (B) pictures,
   - (C) pictures'
   - (D) picture's

GO ON

LANGUAGE: LANGUAGE MECHANICS
SAMPLE TEST (cont.)

For numbers 10–13, read each group of sentences. Find the one that is written correctly and shows the correct capitalization and punctuation.

10.
- (F) How many days do we have until Memorial Day?
- (G) You remind me of my uncle Fester who lives in Bangor Maine.
- (H) "Would you like to go swimming, skating or biking." he asked.
- (J) "I wont go Mr Smith," Doug demanded.

11.
- (A) Do you like french bread, with spaghetti?
- (B) She should be better in a week, but she needs to rest.
- (C) Mrs Patterson the nurse, wont let me go home.
- (D) "After breakfast, said Nina, let's go swimming."

12.
- (F) I love to go for walks, and she likes to ride bikes.
- (G) We went to the mall and bought jeans, and shirts. and shoes.
- (H) "I cant find my homework" said Bill.
- (J) "No? she demanded!

13.
- (A) Breakfast is my favorite meal and Lunch is my least favorite.
- (B) I like to eat eggs bacon, and toast for Breakfast.
- (C) I usually have a boring sandwich for lunch.
- (D) We eat dinner and then we go for a walk!

For numbers 14–17, read the sentence. Fill in the circle beside the answer choice that fits best in the blank and has correct capitalization and punctuation.

14. **Sylvia loves to eat hamburgers with _____**
- (F) french fries.
- (G) French Fries.
- (H) French fries.
- (J) French fries?

15. **In order to do well at a _____ need to practice.**
- (A) sport you
- (B) sport, you
- (C) sport: you
- (D) sport. You

16. **She lives on _____ just two blocks away.**
- (F) Fifth street. Its
- (G) Fifth Street, its
- (H) Fifth Street. It's
- (J) fifth street, it's

17. **_____ showed us how to care for our teeth.**
- (A) Dr. Newman and her assistant
- (B) Dr. Newman, and her assistant
- (C) Dr. Newman and, her assistant,
- (D) Dr. Newman and her Assistant

GO ON

LANGUAGE: LANGUAGE MECHANICS
SAMPLE TEST (cont.)

For numbers 18–21, look at the underlined part of each sentence. Fill in the circle of the choice that shows the correct capitalization and punctuation of the underlined part.

18. Toshi <u>exclaimed we need to start practicing now!</u>"
- Ⓕ exclaimed, we
- Ⓖ exclaimed. We
- Ⓗ exclaimed, "We
- Ⓙ Correct as it is

19. Do you like to travel by <u>bus subway, or car?</u>
- Ⓐ bus, subway,
- Ⓑ bus subway
- Ⓒ bus; subway
- Ⓓ Correct as it is

20. She lives in the small town of <u>Tykesville, Maine.</u>
- Ⓕ Tykesville Maine.
- Ⓖ Tykesville: Maine.
- Ⓗ Tykesville maine:
- Ⓙ Correct as it is

21. "Will you visit <u>Grandma she</u> asked.
- Ⓐ grandma, she
- Ⓑ Grandma," she
- Ⓒ Grandma?" she
- Ⓓ Correct as it is

For numbers 22–25, read the passage. Fill in the circle of the choice that shows the correct capitalization and punctuation for the underlined part.

Annie Oakley was a natural. At the age of nine, she shot a walnut off a tree <u>branch the</u> **(22)** very first time she fired her father's old long-barreled rifle. Her skill with the gun proved a blessing for her <u>family because</u> **(23)** her father had died of a fever when she was <u>four Annie</u> **(24)** helped support her <u>mother brother</u> **(25)** and sisters by shooting and selling quail and rabbits.

22.
- Ⓕ branch, the
- Ⓖ branch. The
- Ⓗ branch; the
- Ⓙ Correct as it is

23.
- Ⓐ family. Because
- Ⓑ family, because
- Ⓒ family; because
- Ⓓ Correct as it is

24.
- Ⓕ four Annie,
- Ⓖ four, Annie
- Ⓗ four. Annie
- Ⓙ Correct as it is

25.
- Ⓐ mother, brother,
- Ⓑ mother brother,
- Ⓒ mother; brother
- Ⓓ Correct as it is

1-57768-976-3 *Spectrum Test Practice 6*

LANGUAGE: LANGUAGE MECHANICS
SAMPLE TEST (cont.)

Read the story and use it to do numbers 26–29.

(1) For many years, people in the United States used streetcars to travel in cities. (2) At first, streetcars were called horse cars because horses pulled them. (3) Later, streetcars were powered by steam in the 1800s, people tried to use electric power, but making electricity was considered to be too expensive. (4) In 1888, a machine was invented that made electricity inexpensively. (5) In that same year, the first electric-powered streetcars were put into use they quickly replaced the steam-powered streetcar. (6) With the invention of the gas engine electric streetcars were soon replaced by buses and cars. (7) By 1930, the streetcar had begun to disappear from city streets. (8) Interest in streetcars revived in the 1970s.

26. In sentence 2, horse cars because is best written —

- (F) horse cars; because
- (G) horse cars, because
- (H) horse cars. Because
- (J) As it is

27. In sentence 3, steam in is best written —

- (A) steam; in
- (B) steam, in
- (C) steam. In
- (D) As it is

28. In sentence 5, use they is best written —

- (F) use: They
- (G) use. They
- (H) use; they
- (J) As it is

29. In sentence 6, gas engine electric is best written —

- (A) gas, engine, electric
- (B) gas, engine electric
- (C) gas engine, electric
- (D) As it is

STOP

LANGUAGE: LANGUAGE EXPRESSION

● Lesson 3: Usage

Directions: Read the directions for each section. Fill in the circle for the answer you think is correct.

Examples

Which word fits best in the sentence?

A.   The volleyball is _____, but she said that you could use it.

- (A) shes
- (B) hers
- (C) her
- (D) thems

Which sentence is complete and correctly written?

B.
- (F) They greets you with flowers and gifts.
- (G) We was going swimming until rain spoiled our plans.
- (H) I come to see you, but you was gone.
- (J) They welcomed us with open arms.

Clue If a question is too difficult, skip it and come back to it later. Before you mark your answer, say it to yourself. Does it sound right?

● Practice

For numbers 1–3, choose the word or phrase that best completes the sentence.

1.   He was _____ at math than his twin.
- (A) best
- (B) better
- (C) more better
- (D) most best

2.   Sally _____ her hair when we arrived.
- (F) cutting
- (G) were cutting
- (H) was cutting
- (J) are cutting

3.   Pizza Shack is _____ favorite restaurant.
- (A) our
- (B) theys
- (C) we
- (D) us

For numbers 4–5, choose the answer that is a complete and correctly written sentence.

4.
- (F) Our class buyed souvenirs in the museum's gift shop.
- (G) My dad and uncle builded the house theyselves.
- (H) We enjoyed our tour of the fire station.
- (J) They was shopping at the mall when they saw him.

5.
- (A) Me and him walked to school together.
- (B) I and Daniel helped Mr. McGinnis paint the walls.
- (C) Marissa and them picked up trash in the playground.
- (D) Angella and I wrote book reports on the same book.

GO ON

LANGUAGE: LANGUAGE EXPRESSION

● **Lesson 3: Usage (cont.)**

For numbers 6–11, read each answer choice. Fill in the space for the choice that has a usage error. If there are no mistakes, fill in the fourth answer space.

6. (F) Meg and I seen
    (G) an accident on the way
    (H) to school this morning.
    (J) No mistakes

7. (A) The driver of a small
    (B) sports car run a stop sign
    (C) and hit a pickup truck.
    (D) No mistakes

8. (F) It's always best
    (G) to obey street signs
    (H) whether you is driving or not.
    (J) No mistakes

9. (A) When Jake grows up,
    (B) he wants to be
    (C) a police officer.
    (D) No mistakes

10. (F) My brother aren't
    (G) feeling well this morning,
    (H) so he isn't going to school.
    (J) No mistakes

11. (A) As she approached,
    (B) we seen that she was
    (C) wearing a new dress.
    (D) No mistakes

For numbers 12 and 13 in the next column, choose the best way to write the underlined part of each sentence. If the underlined part is correct, fill in the circle for the fourth answer.

12. **As we read the story, we began to better <u>understanding</u> why the problem was so complex.**
    (F) understand
    (G) understood
    (H) understands
    (J) No change

13. **<u>However</u> the bus was crowded, she was able to find a seat near the back.**
    (A) Whether
    (B) Although
    (C) Until
    (D) No change

For numbers 14 and 15, choose the answer that is a complete and correctly written sentence.

14. (F) My brother delivering papers every morning before school.
    (G) Has you seen that new TV show yet?
    (H) I think their last album was much more better.
    (J) Bill and Linda were upset with themselves for missing the bus.

15. (A) Jumping up and down with excitement.
    (B) The choir singing the best they ever had.
    (C) He and me will miss you when you're gone.
    (D) Marla twisted her ankle on the ice yesterday.

GO ON

LANGUAGE: LANGUAGE EXPRESSION

● Lesson 3: Usage (cont.)

Read about Abraham Lincoln. Use the passage to do numbers 16–19.

(1) Abraham Lincoln was a poor farm boy, a lawyer, and a congressman. (2) In 1860, he <u>were elected</u> the sixteenth President of the United States.

(3) Whoever first said that anyone could be President was probably thinking of Abraham Lincoln. (4) As a child, Lincoln was highly motivated to learn. (5) He had little formal education, but he educated <u>hisself</u> by reading books by firelight. (6) He believed anyone who gave him a book was a good friend, since <u>books holds</u> the power of knowledge.

(7) Lincoln <u>was always known</u> for his honesty. (8) Before studying law, he was a shopkeeper. (9) He also worked as a postmaster and a store clerk. (10) As President, he not only freed the slaves, but he also proved to be a master statesman and a wise commander-in-chief.

16. In sentence 2, <u>were elected</u> is best written —
    - (F) elected
    - (G) was elected
    - (H) will be elected
    - (J) As it is

17. In sentence 5, <u>hisself</u> is best written —
    - (A) himself
    - (B) theyselves
    - (C) he
    - (D) As it is

18. In sentence 6, <u>books holds</u> is best written —
    - (F) books helds
    - (G) book holds
    - (H) books held
    - (J) As it is

19. In sentence 7, <u>was always known</u> is best written —
    - (A) was always knew
    - (B) always knew
    - (C) is always knew
    - (D) As it is

STOP

LANGUAGE: LANGUAGE EXPRESSION

● Lesson 4: Sentences

Directions: For A, choose the underlined word that is the simple subject of the sentence. For B, choose the underlined word that is the simple predicate (verb) of the sentence. For C, choose the answer that is the best combination of the underlined sentences.

Examples

A. The <u>tiny</u> <u>dog</u> <u>scampered</u> after the
       Ⓐ Ⓑ   Ⓒ
<u>horse</u>.
Ⓓ

B. Three <u>gray</u> <u>crawfish</u> <u>hid</u> under the
      Ⓕ   Ⓖ   Ⓗ
<u>riverbank</u>.
Ⓙ

C. <u>The lake is blue.</u> <u>The lake is warm.</u>

Ⓐ The lake is blue, and it is warm.
Ⓑ The deep warm lake.
Ⓒ The lake is blue and warm.
Ⓓ Blue is the warm lake.

Clue If you are not sure which answer is correct, eliminate answers you know are wrong. Then take your best guess.

● Practice

For numbers 1–3, find the underlined part that is the simple subject of the sentence.

1.   <u>Their</u> <u>cat</u> <u>meowed</u> at the <u>door</u>.
      Ⓐ   Ⓑ   Ⓒ   Ⓓ

2.   The <u>large</u> <u>family</u> <u>picnicked</u> in the <u>city</u> park.
          Ⓕ   Ⓖ   Ⓗ   Ⓙ

3.   <u>Several</u> <u>landmarks</u> <u>helped</u> <u>her</u> to remember the way.
     Ⓐ   Ⓑ   Ⓒ Ⓓ

For numbers 4–6, find the underlined part that is the simple predicate of the sentence.

4.   <u>Omar</u> <u>discovered</u> a <u>snapping</u> turtle in his <u>backyard</u>.
     Ⓕ   Ⓖ   Ⓗ   Ⓙ

5.   Our <u>dad</u> <u>crawled</u> <u>under</u> the sink to <u>fix</u> the leak.
      Ⓐ   Ⓑ   Ⓒ   Ⓓ

6.   Two <u>firemen</u> <u>visited</u> our <u>classroom</u> to <u>talk</u> about their jobs.
       Ⓕ   Ⓖ   Ⓗ   Ⓙ

GO ON

Name _____   Date _____

● **Lesson 4: Sentences (cont.)**

For numbers 7–9, choose the answer that best combines the underlined sentences.

7. <u>Mr. Norton called this morning.</u>
   <u>Mr. Norton said his wife is sick.</u>

   (A) Mr. Norton called this morning and Mr. Norton said his wife is sick.

   (B) Mr. Norton called this morning, and he said his wife is sick.

   (C) This morning, Mr. Norton called and said his wife is sick.

   (D) Mr. Norton called this morning to say his wife is sick.

8. <u>George left early.</u>
   <u>Carol left early.</u>
   <u>They are going to the band festival.</u>

   (F) George and Carol left early because to the band festival they are going.

   (G) George and Carol left early to go to the band festival.

   (H) George left early and Carol because they are going to the band festival.

   (J) Leaving early, George and Carol are going to the band festival.

9. <u>The birds sing beautifully.</u>
   <u>The birds are in the tree.</u>

   (A) The birds are in the tree, and they sing beautifully.

   (B) The birds, in the tree, singing beautifully.

   (C) The birds sing beautifully and are in the tree.

   (D) The birds in the tree sing beautifully.

For numbers 10 and 11, choose the best way of expressing the idea.

10. (F) Because year after year, the salmon struggle upstream to spawn.

    (G) Upstream to spawn, the salmon struggle year after year.

    (H) Year after year, the salmon struggle upstream to spawn.

    (J) The salmon struggle year after year upstream to spawn.

11. (A) The plumber fixed the pipe because it was leaking.

    (B) The plumber fixed the leaking pipe.

    (C) Because the pipe was leaking, the plumber fixed the pipe.

    (D) The pipe was leaking, and the plumber fixed the pipe.

GO ON

LANGUAGE: LANGUAGE EXPRESSION

● Lesson 4: Sentences (cont.)

Read about one town's centennial celebration. Use the story to do numbers 12–15.

(1) Last May our centennial anniversary for our town was celebrated by us. (2) We made a lot of preparations. (3) A cleanup committee washed all public buildings.
(4) They also brushed all public buildings.
(5) Members of the fire department climbed on high ladders to hang up flags and bunting.

(6) At last the celebration began. (7) The high point was when Mayor Lopez asked Olga Janssen—at 105, our oldest citizen—what she remembered about the old days. (8) Mrs. Janssen recalled how her mother had used a churn to make butter, and her favorite memory was of playing dominoes with her cousins.

(9) At the end, we all drank a ginger ale toast to the town's next century. (10) We knew most of us would not be here for the next celebration, but we felt happy to be at this one. (11) A large bell was struck with a mallet by the mayor to officially close our celebration.

12. How is sentence 1 best written?

- (F) Last May our town's centennial anniversary was celebrated by us.
- (G) Last May, we celebrated our town's centennial anniversary.
- (H) We celebrated last May our town's centennial anniversary.
- (J) As it is

13. How are sentences 3 and 4 best combined?

- (A) A cleanup committee washed all public buildings and then brushed them.
- (B) A cleanup committee washed, and they also brushed, all public buildings.
- (C) A cleanup committee washed and brushed all public buildings.
- (D) As it is

14. Sentence 11 is best written —

- (F) The mayor officially closed our celebration with a mallet by striking a large bell.
- (G) Striking a large bell with a mallet, our celebration officially closed by the mayor.
- (H) To officially close our celebration, the mayor struck a large bell with a mallet.
- (J) As it is

15. Which sentence should be broken into two sentences?

- (A) 2
- (B) 5
- (C) 8
- (D) 10

STOP

Name _____ Date_____

LANGUAGE: LANGUAGE EXPRESSION

● Lesson 5: Paragraphs

Directions: Read the directions for each section. Fill in the circle for the answer you think is correct.

Example

Read the paragraph below. Find the best topic sentence for the paragraph.

    A. _____. Some you can pick up and perhaps even take home for pets. But would you believe a lizard exists that can grow up to 10 feet long and weigh 300 pounds. Now, that's a lizard!

Ⓐ My favorite pets are dogs.

Ⓑ Some lizards are cute little reptiles no more than a few centimeters in length.

Ⓒ Do you think dinosaurs were the ancestors of reptiles or birds?

Ⓓ Would you like to have a lizard as a pet?

 Clue

Stay with your first answer choice. You should change an answer only if you are sure it is incorrect. Remember, a paragraph should focus on one idea. The correct answer is the one that fits best with the rest of the paragraph.

● Practice

Read the paragraph below. Find the best topic sentence for the paragraph.

    1. _____. Ants that live in sandy places such as dunes and deserts are plagued by the larvae of two insects. These larvae ambush their prey from concealed sand traps. One of these insects is the tiger beetle. The other is the ant lion.

Ⓐ People have lots of troubles.

Ⓑ Ants are part of the insect family.

Ⓒ Ants can have problems.

Ⓓ Like bees, ants live in a very complex social system.

Find the answer choice that best develops the topic sentence below.

2.   The sod houses of the Great Plains had their drawbacks.

Ⓕ They were fireproof, windproof, and, for the most part, bulletproof.

Ⓖ During heavy rains, the roof leaked, and water and mud dripped into whatever happened to be cooking on the stove.

Ⓗ Most were built so strong that they could withstand tornadoes and snowstorms.

Ⓙ The sod house was home to most of those hardy souls who braved life on the Great Plains.

 GO ON

LANGUAGE: LANGUAGE EXPRESSION

● **Lesson 5: Paragraphs (cont.)**

For numbers 3 and 4, read the paragraph. Find the sentence that does not belong in the paragraph.

3. **(1)** Canada is more than a land of great beauty. **(2)** It borders the United States to the south. **(3)** It is also a land of vast forests. **(4)** Lumber and the products that come from lumber make Canada a leader in world paper production. **(5)** The pulp and paper industry continues to grow and is now Canada's leading industry.

- Ⓐ Sentence 2
- Ⓑ Sentence 3
- Ⓒ Sentence 4
- Ⓓ Sentence 5

4. **(1)** The most beautiful of all horses is the Arabian Asil. **(2)** Its neck is gracefully arched. **(3)** Its head is small and delicate with eyes that are large, fiery, and far apart. **(4)** Its small ears point inward. **(5)** This horse is well noted for its endurance. **(6)** The horse has a full, flowing tail, and its skin is a shiny black.

- Ⓕ Sentence 2
- Ⓖ Sentence 4
- Ⓗ Sentence 5
- Ⓙ Sentence 6

For numbers 5 and 6, read the paragraph. Find the sentence that best fits the blank in the paragraph.

5. He was greeted by enthusiastic crowds in Paris and London. When he returned to the United States, he was given one of the largest ticker-tape parades in New York history. Overnight, his name became a household word. _____. Aviator Douglas Corrigan, who, following a most unusual feat, was known worldwide as Wrong-Way Corrigan.

- Ⓐ Whether it was legitimate or not, Douglas Corrigan's flight made him famous.
- Ⓑ His ideas were as well known as the President's.
- Ⓒ Who was this new American hero?
- Ⓓ Where did this man call his home?

6. In 1937, Douglas Corrigan had requested permission to fly over the Atlantic to Europe. His request was denied after federal aviation officials inspected his plane. _____. One tank was even located directly in front of the pilot's seat and nearly blocked Corrigan's vision.

- Ⓕ His plane did not have the capacity to hold enough fuel to cross the ocean.
- Ⓖ Corrigan had added so many extra gas tanks to his dilapidated craft that it was considered a deathtrap.
- Ⓗ Authorities feared Corrigan would run out of fuel with no land in sight.
- Ⓙ His plane had no added room for extra supplies of food and water.

GO ON

● **Lesson 5: Paragraphs (cont.)**

For numbers 7–9, use the paragraph below to answer the questions.

(1) "This is a pretty good poem," she thought to herself. (2) "It's just that . . . " (3) Lois wondered if she had fed her dog before she left for school. (4) Then her name was called, she stood up, and her knees began to shake. (5) When she turned around and looked at the rest of the class, however, she saw friendly faces.

7. Choose the best first sentence for this paragraph.

Ⓐ Lois waited for her turn to read her poem in front of the class.

Ⓑ Lois could hardly wait to go to lunch.

Ⓒ Lois was looking forward to reading her play.

Ⓓ Lois loved English class.

8. Which sentence should be left out of this paragraph?

Ⓕ Sentence 1

Ⓖ Sentence 2

Ⓗ Sentence 3

Ⓙ Sentence 5

9. Choose the last sentence for this paragraph.

Ⓐ "Oh, no," she remembered, "I didn't feed the dog."

Ⓑ Lois felt like running from the room.

Ⓒ Lois decided that this would be a great time to read all of her poems.

Ⓓ "Maybe this won't be so bad after all," Lois thought with relief.

10. Which of the following would be most appropriate in a letter asking permission to hold a car wash in a store's parking lot?

Ⓕ Your store is the best grocery store in Orchard Grove. My parents buy all their groceries at your store. Our class is trying to raise money for a class trip. We would like to hold a car wash in your parking lot on Saturday, because we would get lots of business on that day.

Ⓖ We have 25 students in our class. Our teacher's name is Mr. Wordsworth. He is a great teacher. He said I should write to ask if we could hold a car wash in your parking lot on Saturday. He thought you would say yes.

Ⓗ The students in our class are raising money for our class trip. We would like your permission to hold a car wash in your parking lot on Saturday from 9:00 A.M. to 3 P.M. We promise to clean up when we are finished. We appreciate your consideration of this matter.

Ⓙ The students in our class think the best place to have a car wash would be in your parking lot. We think we could raise lots of money there. We need money to go on a class trip, since the school will not pay our way. Saturday from 9:00 A.M. to 3 P.M. would be a great time for us.

GO ON

LANGUAGE: LANGUAGE EXPRESSION

● **Lesson 5: Paragraphs (cont.)**

Read this story about Amelia Earhart. Use the story to answer questions 11–14.

(1) <u>The weather was bad</u> over the mid-Atlantic Ocean. (2) The small plane's engine sputtered. (3) The slim, young woman at the controls knew she was too far out to turn back. (4) Carefully she coaxed the plane ahead through the storm.

(5) When dawn came, the engine was failing seriously. (6) Just ahead lay the Irish coast. (7) As the engine gasped its last breath, the woman brought her plane down in a cow pasture. (8) An astonished farmer raced over as the young woman climbed out of the airplane. (9) "I'm from America," she said. (10) "My name is Amelia Earhart." (11) The farmer was angry that she had ruined part of his field. (12) She had even set a new speed record: thirteen hours and thirty minutes!

(13) They didn't think a woman was strong enough to keep going through the long night. (14) However, Earhart had strength and courage to spare. (15) She had already made parachute jumps and had explored the ocean floor in a diver's suit. (16) Now, overnight, she had become famous.

11. Which sentence could be added after sentence 10?

- Ⓐ The farmer thought she was an alien from outer space.
- Ⓑ She had become the first woman to fly over the Atlantic Ocean alone.
- Ⓒ She had become the first woman to safely land in a pasture.
- Ⓓ She added, "Do you know where I might get something good to eat?"

12. Which sentence could begin the third paragraph?

- Ⓕ Many people had told Amelia not to make this flight.
- Ⓖ Amelia wanted to give up.
- Ⓗ Amelia was a weak woman.
- Ⓙ Amelia loved to set world records.

13. Which group of words would be more colorful than the underlined words in sentence 1?

- Ⓐ There was lightning
- Ⓑ Lightning ripped through the blackness
- Ⓒ It was cold and wet
- Ⓓ The weather was stormy

14. Which sentence does not belong in the story?

- Ⓕ Sentence 2
- Ⓖ Sentence 6
- Ⓗ Sentence 11
- Ⓙ Sentence 16

LANGUAGE: LANGUAGE EXPRESSION
SAMPLE TEST

● **Directions:** Read the directions, and then fill in the circle of the correct answer.

Example

Find the underlined part that is the simple predicate (verb) of the sentence.

E1. The gray kangaroo leaped across our path.
      (A)   (B)   (C)   (D)

For number 1, choose the word or phrase that best completes the sentence.

1. Last week, my family _____ our relatives in Grand Rapids, Michigan.

    (A) visit
    (B) will visit
    (C) visited
    (D) visits

For number 2, choose the answer that is a complete and correctly written sentence.

2. (F) I was very pleased with the band's performance.
    (G) We is going to Greenfield Village on Saturday.
    (H) My mom takes me shopping to buy new clothes yesterday.
    (J) Please help she clean your room.

For numbers 3–5, read each answer choice. Fill in the circle for the choice that has a usage error. If there is no mistake, fill in the fourth answer space.

3. (A) I'm wondering if I will ever
    (B) finish this book. I were supposed
    (C) to have it completed today.
    (D) No mistake

4. (F) Amanda give her report
    (G) on hedgehogs. Ali gave
    (H) his report on chimpanzees.
    (J) No mistake

5. (A) We don't never get to go
    (B) to the movies. Does your
    (C) family go often?
    (D) No mistake

For number 6, find the underlined part that is the simple subject of the sentence.

6. Green iguanas are Alexander's favorite
         (F)   (G)   (H)
    type of pet.
    (J)

For number 7, find the underlined part that is the simple predicate of the sentence.

7. An editor from a local publishing
          (A)
    company spoke to our class on Monday.
       (B)   (C)   (D)

GO ON

LANGUAGE: LANGUAGE EXPRESSION
SAMPLE TEST (cont.)

For numbers 8–10, choose the answer that best combines the underlined sentences.

8. **Gordon is going to the store.**
   Samantha is going with him.
   - (F) Gordon is going to the store and so is Samantha.
   - (G) Gordon and Samantha are going to the store.
   - (H) To the store, Gordon and Samantha are going.
   - (J) Gordon and Samantha to the store are going.

9. **Please go to the refrigerator.**
   I would like you to get a soda for me.
   - (A) Please go to the refrigerator to get me a soda.
   - (B) Please go to the refrigerator to get me a soda, because I want one.
   - (C) For me, please go to the refrigerator to get a soda.
   - (D) I would like for you to please go to the refrigerator to get a soda for me.

10. **Ms. Lightfoot loves dancing.**
    She goes to the dance studio every day.
    She goes at eight o'clock.
    - (F) Ms. Lightfoot loves dancing, and she goes to the dance studio every day at eight o'clock.
    - (G) Ms. Lightfoot goes to the dance studio every day at eight o'clock, because she loves dancing.
    - (H) Ms. Lightfoot loves dancing every day at the studio at eight o'clock.
    - (J) Every day, Ms. Lightfoot loves going to the dance studio to dance at eight o'clock.

For numbers 11 and 12, choose the best way of expressing the idea.

11.
   - (A) In the family room is our television, which we enjoy together as a family.
   - (B) Our television is in the family room, which my family enjoys together.
   - (C) My family enjoys watching television together in the family room.
   - (D) My family enjoys in the family room watching television.

12.
   - (F) Because of the heavy rain, we had to take a detour the police officer said.
   - (G) The police officer said because of the heavy rain, we had to take a detour.
   - (H) The police officer told us to take a detour because of the heavy rain.
   - (J) We had to take a detour, said the police officer, in spite of the heavy rain.

LANGUAGE: LANGUAGE EXPRESSION
SAMPLE TEST (cont.)

Read the paragraph below. Find the best topic sentence for the paragraph.

13. _____. When you first begin, all that comes out are high-pitched squeaks. Before long, you can play a simple melody. Eventually, playing your instrument is almost second nature.

- (A) Learning to ride a bike is a long process.
- (B) Playing a clarinet takes time and practice.
- (C) Playing a clarinet is simple.
- (D) Becoming a concert pianist is difficult.

Find the answer choice that best develops the topic sentence.

14. **White-water rafting is a thrilling but dangerous sport.**
- (F) Meandering through forests and observing the wildlife is very relaxing.
- (G) Steering the raft together is great teamwork.
- (H) The water can be cold, so dress appropriately.
- (J) If you fall overboard, you can be dashed against the rocks.

Read the paragraph below. Find the sentence that does not fit in the paragraph.

15. **(1)** Remember when you were just three or four years old, and you pulled out crayons and paper and wrote Grandma a letter? **(2)** Grandma lived far away. **(3)** You drew circles and lines. **(4)** Perhaps you drew a loopy script that looked more like art than writing. **(5)** When you gave the note to Grandma, she let you read it aloud. **(6)** It may have seemed like a game, but the truth is that you were really practicing an important step in writing.

- (A) Sentence 1
- (B) Sentence 2
- (C) Sentence 3
- (D) Sentence 6

Read the paragraph below. Find the sentence that best fits the blank in the paragraph.

16. The Internet can be a great resource for research papers. _____. When doing a research paper, be sure to check facts with several reliable sources. Never rely on one source.

- (F) When visiting chat rooms, never supply any personal information, such as your name or telephone number.
- (G) Use a filter to screen out objectionable sites.
- (H) Search for sites associated with organizations and institutions.
- (J) Never give out your parent's credit card number.

GO ON

LANGUAGE: LANGUAGE EXPRESSION
SAMPLE TEST (cont.)

Read more about the steps involved in writing. Use the passage to answer numbers 17–20.

(1) Years ago people believed that children could not write until they could spell. (2) Children practiced letters or were given spelling words or dictation to copy, but schools did not consider scribbling to be writing. (3) Children in early elementary school spent their time painting or playing with blocks or clay. (4) Scribbling then was just scribbling.

(5) Teachers now <u>believes, that encouraging</u> young children to scribble is an important step in writing. (6) Teachers have discovered that it is important for children to write before they even know their alphabet. (7) Young children encouraged to write lists and tell stories, leave messages and make signs. (8) They should be asked to read their writing aloud, although unreadable it may be.

17. Which sentence should be added after sentence 5?

- (A) Recess was my favorite activity of the day.
- (B) This early writing may not be readable, but it is still writing.
- (C) Playing dress up and other play activities also are beneficial.
- (D) Naptime is a necessary part of the young child's day.

18. How is sentence 8 best written?

- (F) Even because it is unreadable, they should be asked to read their writing aloud.
- (G) They should be asked to read their writing aloud, even if it is unreadable.
- (H) Because they should be asked to read their unreadable writing aloud.
- (J) As it is

19. Which group of words is not a complete thought?

- (A) Sentence 2
- (B) Sentence 3
- (C) Sentence 7
- (D) Sentence 8

20. In sentence 5, <u>believes, that encouraging</u> is best written —

- (F) believe that encouraging
- (G) believe. That encouraging
- (H) believe that, encouraging
- (J) As it is

STOP

Name _____   Date_____

LANGUAGE: SPELLING

● Lesson 6: Spelling Skills

Directions: Follow the directions for each section. Choose the answer you think is correct.

Examples

Find the word that is spelled correctly and fits best in the sentence.

A.   The boat _____ toward shore.
- (A) driffed
- (B) drifded
- (C) drifted
- (D) drifteded

One of the underlined words is misspelled. Which answer choice is spelled incorrectly?

B.
- (F) great <u>honor</u>
- (G) <u>ackward</u> moment
- (H) <u>bald</u> eagle
- (J) dark <u>alley</u>

 Clue Read the directions carefully. Be sure you know if you should look for the correctly spelled word or the incorrectly spelled word.

● Practice

For numbers 1–5, find the word that is spelled correctly and fits best in the blank.

1.   _____ of the dog!
- (A) Beaware
- (B) Beware
- (C) Bewear
- (D) Bewaar

2.   The _____ hit the moon.
- (F) asteroid
- (G) astroid
- (H) asterood
- (J) asteruod

3.   He spoke with a _____ accent.
- (A) gutteral
- (B) gutterle
- (C) guttural
- (D) gutural

4.   My favorite _____ is lemonade.
- (F) beaverage
- (G) beverage
- (H) bevirage
- (J) bevarage

5.   The forest was _____ with color.
- (A) ablase
- (B) ableaze
- (C) ablaze
- (D) abblaze

For numbers 6–8, read the phrases. Choose the phrase in which the underlined word is not spelled correctly.

6.
- (F) <u>horizontle</u> line
- (G) <u>install</u> software
- (H) <u>graham</u> cracker
- (J) firm <u>mattress</u>

7.
- (A) <u>invisible</u> man
- (B) <u>covert</u> operation
- (C) glove <u>compartmant</u>
- (D) <u>contagious</u> disease

8.
- (F) our <u>forfathers</u>
- (G) <u>burlap</u> sack
- (H) <u>hither</u> and yon
- (J) graduating <u>senior</u>

 GO ON

LANGUAGE: SPELLING

● Lesson 6: Spelling Skills (cont.)

For numbers 9–11, read each answer. Fill in the space for the choice that has a spelling error. If there is no mistake, fill in the last answer choice.

9. Ⓐ veer
    Ⓑ usher
    Ⓒ surplus
    Ⓓ No mistakes

10. Ⓕ smack
    Ⓖ stitch
    Ⓗ toppel
    Ⓙ No mistakes

11. Ⓐ patter
    Ⓑ schedulle
    Ⓒ mute
    Ⓓ No mistakes

For numbers 12–14, read each phrase. One of the underlined words is not spelled correctly for the way it is used in the phrase. Fill in the circle for the word that is not spelled correctly.

12. Ⓕ a flare for fashion
    Ⓖ bottle cork
    Ⓗ hunker down
    Ⓙ internal medicine

13. Ⓐ sentence fragment
    Ⓑ the earth's corps
    Ⓒ cancel an appointment
    Ⓓ leaky faucet

14. Ⓕ subtle hint
    Ⓖ sensible plan
    Ⓗ except an offer
    Ⓙ food staples

For numbers 15–18, find the underlined word that is misspelled. If all the words are spelled correctly, fill in the circle for No mistake.

15. The abilitie to read is a vital skill for
    Ⓐ   Ⓑ   Ⓒ
    all. No mistake.
    Ⓓ

16. The surly usher sneered at the boy.
    Ⓕ   Ⓖ   Ⓗ
    No mistake.
    Ⓙ

17. Dr. McCoy played billiards in the
    Ⓐ
    lounge with a formidible opponent.
    Ⓑ   Ⓒ
    No mistake.
    Ⓓ

18. The abbot in the abbie sings alto.
    Ⓕ   Ⓖ   Ⓗ
    No mistake.
    Ⓙ

STOP

Name _____ Date_____

LANGUAGE: SPELLING
SAMPLE TEST

● **Directions:** For E1, find the word that shows the correct spelling and fits best in the sentence. For E2, look for the underlined word that has a spelling mistake.

Examples

E1. Ellen _____ for losing her temper.
- Ⓐ apologised
- Ⓑ apologized
- Ⓒ aplogized
- Ⓓ appologized

E2.
- Ⓕ befriend the new student
- Ⓖ speak on your behalf
- Ⓗ Vietnam veteren
- Ⓙ snug in bed

For numbers 1–6, find the word that is spelled correctly and fits best in the blank.

1. Can I have your _____?
- Ⓐ autograff
- Ⓑ autograph
- Ⓒ ottograff
- Ⓓ oatograph

2. Do not cross the _____.
- Ⓕ burrier
- Ⓖ barriere
- Ⓗ barrier
- Ⓙ burier

3. My mother loves to shop for _____.
- Ⓐ antigues
- Ⓑ antikes
- Ⓒ anticues
- Ⓓ antiques

4. Do you have any _____ foil?
- Ⓕ alluminum
- Ⓖ aluminum
- Ⓗ alloominem
- Ⓙ aluminem

5. He was very _____.
- Ⓐ purplexed
- Ⓑ purplecked
- Ⓒ perplexed
- Ⓓ perplecked

6. My brother has to use an inhaler for his _____.
- Ⓕ asma
- Ⓖ asthma
- Ⓗ asthme
- Ⓙ ashma

For numbers 7–10, read the phrases. Choose the phrase in which the underlined word is not spelled correctly.

7.
- Ⓐ sit on the balcony
- Ⓑ the abominible snowman
- Ⓒ alkaline battery
- Ⓓ the dog yelped

8.
- Ⓕ apology accepted
- Ⓖ filled with awe
- Ⓗ dispise spiders
- Ⓙ jostled in the crowd

9.
- Ⓐ our residance
- Ⓑ adhesive tape
- Ⓒ compose a sonnet
- Ⓓ nouns and adjectives

10.
- Ⓕ cast your ballot
- Ⓖ buy a trinkette
- Ⓗ drive the vehicle
- Ⓙ play the lyre

GO ON

LANGUAGE: SPELLING
SAMPLE TEST (cont.)

For numbers 11–13, read each answer. Fill in the space for the choice that has a spelling error. If there is no mistake, fill in the circle for the last answer.

11.
- Ⓐ aristocrat
- Ⓑ trespass
- Ⓒ gleeming
- Ⓓ No mistake.

12.
- Ⓕ acsess
- Ⓖ bluff
- Ⓗ valve
- Ⓙ No mistake.

13.
- Ⓐ ardent
- Ⓑ tripod
- Ⓒ tongue
- Ⓓ No mistake.

For numbers 14–16, read each phrase. One of the underlined words is not spelled correctly for the way it is used in the phrase. Fill in the circle for the word that is not spelled correctly.

14.
- Ⓕ brief incident
- Ⓖ peal the potatoes
- Ⓗ a bonnie belle
- Ⓙ dance the waltz

15.
- Ⓐ pore the milk
- Ⓑ grammar skills
- Ⓒ vile behavior
- Ⓓ wash with ammonia

16.
- Ⓕ hold for ransom
- Ⓖ read the text
- Ⓗ serf the waves
- Ⓙ call a truce

For numbers 17–20, find the underlined part that is misspelled. If all the words are spelled correctly, fill in the circle for No mistake.

17. Please discard your uneaten sereal in
    Ⓐ   Ⓑ
    the garbage disposal. No mistake.
    Ⓒ   Ⓓ

18. The twins were dressed in identical
    Ⓕ
    khaki pants and calico shirts.
    Ⓖ   Ⓗ
    No mistake.
    Ⓙ

19. You are indispensible in your capacity
    Ⓐ   Ⓑ
    as class secretary. No mistake.
    Ⓒ   Ⓓ

20. Please don't fling gruel or grapple
    Ⓕ   Ⓖ   Ⓗ
    with your brother. No mistake.
    Ⓙ

STOP

Name _____ Date _____

Lesson 7: Study Skills

Directions: Follow the directions for each section. Choose the answer you think is correct.

Example

Table of Contents	
Chapter	**Page**
1 The First Automobiles 1	
2 Automobiles in America 15	
3 Automobiles Today 24	
4 Choosing an Automobile 30	

A. **If you wanted to buy an automobile, on what pages would you look?**

- (A) pages 1–14
- (B) pages 15–23
- (C) pages 24–29
- (D) pages 30 and following

 Clue If you are not sure which answer is correct, eliminate choices you know are wrong and then take your best guess.

Practice

The illustration below shows a set of encyclopedias. Each of the numbered volumes holds information about topics that begin with the letters shown on that volume. Use the picture to do numbers 1 and 2.

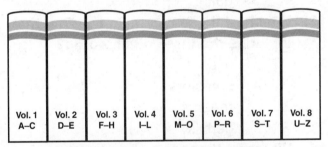

| Vol. 1 A–C | Vol. 2 D–E | Vol. 3 F–H | Vol. 4 I–L | Vol. 5 M–O | Vol. 6 P–R | Vol. 7 S–T | Vol. 8 U–Z |

1. **Which volume would provide information about frogs and toads?**
   - (A) Volume 1
   - (B) Volume 4
   - (C) Volume 6
   - (D) Volume 8

2. **Which volume would include information on opossums and kangaroos?**
   - (F) Volume 2
   - (G) Volume 5
   - (H) Volume 7
   - (J) Volume 8

Use this part of a page from a telephone book to answer numbers 3 and 4.

Salinsky, Paul   107 Prior Lane 788-8789
Samson, Saul   123 Road Way 798-5434
Simpson, Susan   778 Apple Road 799-2229
Smith, Charles   5555 Oak Avenue 768-8992
Smith, Chuck   111 Prior Lane 788-5456
Soldez, Maria   3579 River Road 779-1133

3. **Where does Maria Soldez live?**
   - (A) 107 Prior Lane
   - (B) 778 Apple Road
   - (C) 5555 Oak Avenue
   - (D) 3579 River Road

4. **Paul Salinsky lives very near —**
   - (F) Saul Samson
   - (G) Charles Smith
   - (H) Chuck Smith
   - (J) Susan Simpson

LANGUAGE: STUDY SKILLS

● Lesson 7: Study Skills (cont.)

Use this card from a library card catalog to do numbers 5–8.

```
693.2
       GROUCHO MARX

920    Blue, Alicia
Marx   One Funny Family / by Alicia
       Blue. Photographs by Comedians
       Archives. Cleveland: Dianson
       Publishing Company, 1974.
       244 p.; photos; 24 cm

       1. Marx, Julius "Groucho"   2. Comedians,
       American  3. Movies, Comedies   I. Title
```

5. **From this library catalog card, you know that Groucho Marx is —**
   - Ⓐ the author
   - Ⓑ the publisher
   - Ⓒ a comedian
   - Ⓓ a photographer

6. **What is the title of this book?**
   - Ⓕ Groucho Marx
   - Ⓖ One Funny Family
   - Ⓗ American Comedians
   - Ⓙ Blue, Alicia

7. **In which section of the card catalog would this card be found?**
   - Ⓐ Title
   - Ⓑ Subject
   - Ⓒ Publisher
   - Ⓓ Author

8. **From where did the photographs for this book come?**
   - Ⓕ Dianson Publishing Company
   - Ⓖ Alicia Blue
   - Ⓗ Groucho Marx
   - Ⓙ Comedians Archives

Read each question below. Mark the space for the answer you think is correct.

9. **Look at these guidewords from a dictionary page.** | molehill—monad |

   Which word could be found on the page?
   - Ⓐ molecule
   - Ⓑ mollusk
   - Ⓒ monarch
   - Ⓓ mold

10. **Look at these guidewords from a dictionary page.** | guess—guile |

    Which word could be found on the page?
    - Ⓕ guerilla
    - Ⓖ guffaw
    - Ⓗ gulp
    - Ⓙ guitar

11. **Which of these is a main heading that includes the three other words?**
    - Ⓐ mice
    - Ⓑ hamsters
    - Ⓒ rodents
    - Ⓓ gerbils

12. **Which of these is a main heading that includes the three other words?**
    - Ⓕ tornadoes
    - Ⓖ hurricanes
    - Ⓗ earthquakes
    - Ⓙ natural disasters

13. **If these places were organized from largest to smallest, what would be first?**
    - Ⓐ village
    - Ⓑ city
    - Ⓒ town
    - Ⓓ state

STOP

Name _____   Date_____

LANGUAGE: STUDY SKILLS
SAMPLE TEST

● **Directions:** Read each question. Mark the answer that you think is correct.

E1. Where could you find out how to break the word *parachute* into syllables?
- Ⓐ an atlas
- Ⓑ an encyclopedia
- Ⓒ a dictionary
- Ⓓ an almanac

E2. Which of these would probably appear in the index of a book about flight?
- Ⓕ Chapter 3, Ford's Model T
- Ⓖ Chapter 2, Earhart's Ocean Flight
- Ⓗ *The Wright Brothers* by Arnold Snoazer
- Ⓙ jets, 449–557

Saleem is writing a report about orangutans. He began by making the web below. Use it to do numbers 1–4.

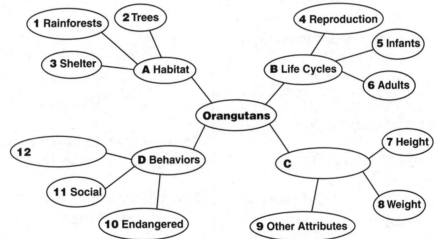

1. Which of these should go in circle C?
   - Ⓐ Physical Characteristics
   - Ⓑ Lifestyles
   - Ⓒ Coloration
   - Ⓓ Arm Spans

2. Which idea in Saleem's web does not belong?
   - Ⓕ 2
   - Ⓖ 6
   - Ⓗ 9
   - Ⓙ 10

3. Which of these belongs in circle 12?
   - Ⓐ Culture
   - Ⓑ Communication
   - Ⓒ Sports
   - Ⓓ Religion

4. If Saleem wanted to add a circle E to the web, which of these would be best?
   - Ⓕ Diet
   - Ⓖ Education
   - Ⓗ Pastimes
   - Ⓙ Beliefs

GO ON

Study this table of the wars in which the United States was involved. It lists the wars, the years the United States was involved, and the Presidents who were in office during these wars. Then do numbers 5–8.

War	Dates	President(s)
War of 1812	1812–1815	Madison
Mexican War	1846–1848	Polk
Civil War	1861–1865	Lincoln
Spanish American War	1898	McKinley
World War I	1914–1918	Wilson
World War II	1941–1945	F. Roosevelt, Truman
Korean War	1950–1953	Truman, Eisenhower
Vietnam War	1965–1973	Johnson, Nixon
Persian Gulf War	1991	G. Bush

5. **Which of these wars was the earliest?**
   - (A) Persian Gulf War
   - (B) Civil War
   - (C) War of 1812
   - (D) Spanish American War

6. **Which war was the longest?**
   - (F) World War I
   - (G) Vietnam War
   - (H) War of 1812
   - (J) Mexican War

7. **Which President was in office during two wars?**
   - (A) Madison
   - (B) Nixon
   - (C) Truman
   - (D) Wilson

8. **Which war was the most recent?**
   - (F) World War II
   - (G) Persian Gulf War
   - (H) Vietnam War
   - (J) Korean War

For numbers 9–11, choose the word that would appear first if the words were arranged in alphabetical order.

9.
   - (A) tablet
   - (B) tableau
   - (C) tabard
   - (D) tabulate

10.
   - (F) regret
   - (G) regress
   - (H) rekindle
   - (J) reinforce

11.
   - (A) Roberts, Kevin
   - (B) Roberts, Cynthia
   - (C) Roberts, Candy
   - (D) Roberts, Clifford

For numbers 12 and 13, choose the best source of information.

12. **Which of these would tell you the names of the rivers in Africa?**
   - (F) an atlas
   - (G) a thesaurus
   - (H) a dictionary
   - (J) a book of quotations

13. **Which of these would help you to decide which lizard would be the best pet for you?**
   - (A) an encyclopedia
   - (B) a gardening book
   - (C) a handbook on lizards
   - (D) a dictionary

GO ON

LANGUAGE: STUDY SKILLS
SAMPLE TEST (cont.)

Use the Table of Contents and Index below to answer numbers 14–18. They are from a book on science questions and answers.

Table of Contents

Chapter		Page
	Questions	
1	The Natural World	3
2	The Human Body	33
3	The Home Planet	59
4	Numbers and Formulas	71
	Answers	
5	The Natural World	105
6	The Human Body	155
7	The Home Planet	203
8	Numbers and Formulas	227

Index

antibodies, 50, 188
ants, 3, 105
aspirin, 41, 170
bats, 30, 151
Big Dipper, 143
brain, 171
calcium, 53, 193
centipedes, 21, 136
color, 92, 189
digestion, 130–131, 166
dolphins, 14, 124
   bottlenose, 30, 124, 151
doves, mourning, 12, 120
eardrums, 179
evergreens, 8
fever, 170, 182
food allergies, 39, 167
hay fever, 163
hurricanes, 60, 205, 206
insect bites, 48, 183
jet engine, 239–240
kerosene, 222
leap years, 255
lips, 179

14. In which chapter would you probably find a question about the liver's function?
    - (F) Chapter 1
    - (G) Chapter 2
    - (H) Chapter 4
    - (J) Chapter 6

15. From looking at the table of contents and index, which of the topics below would most likely be covered in chapters 1 and 5?
    - (A) mumps and measles
    - (B) plants and animals
    - (C) earthquakes
    - (D) helicopters

16. On which page might you find an answer about why your face turns red when you perspire?
    - (F) Page 7
    - (G) Page 38
    - (H) Page 65
    - (J) Page 157

17. Which of these topics is found in chapter 3?
    - (A) jet engine
    - (B) hay fever
    - (C) hurricanes
    - (D) lips

18. From looking at the index and table of contents, who would most likely be interested in this book?
    - (F) someone who loves to read novels
    - (G) someone who enjoys science trivia
    - (H) someone who wants to know how to build a tree house
    - (J) someone who wants to plant a garden

STOP

ANSWER SHEET

STUDENT'S NAME

LAST · FIRST · MI

(Bubble grid A–Z for each letter column)

SCHOOL

TEACHER

FEMALE ◯ MALE ◯

BIRTH DATE

MONTH	DAY	YEAR
JAN ◯	0 0	0
FEB ◯	1 1	1
MAR ◯	2 2	2
APR ◯	3 3	3
MAY ◯	4	4
JUN ◯	5	5 5
JUL ◯	6	6 6
AUG ◯	7	7 7
SEP ◯	8	8 8
OCT ◯	9	9 9
NOV ◯		0
DEC ◯		

GRADE
⑤ ⑥ ⑦

Part 4: STUDY SKILLS

E1 (A) (B) (C) (D)
1 (A) (B) (C) (D)
2 (F) (G) (H) (J)
3 (A) (B) (C) (D)
4 (F) (G) (H) (J)
5 (A) (B) (C) (D)
6 (F) (G) (H) (J)
7 (A) (B) (C) (D)
8 (F) (G) (H) (J)
9 (A) (B) (C) (D)
10 (F) (G) (H) (J)

Part 1: LANGUAGE MECHANICS

E1 (A) (B) (C) (D)
1 (A) (B) (C) (D)
2 (F) (G) (H) (J)
3 (A) (B) (C) (D)
4 (F) (G) (H) (J)
5 (A) (B) (C) (D)
6 (F) (G) (H) (J)
7 (A) (B) (C) (D)
8 (F) (G) (H) (J)
9 (A) (B) (C) (D)
10 (F) (G) (H) (J)
11 (A) (B) (C) (D)
12 (F) (G) (H) (J)
13 (A) (B) (C) (D)
14 (F) (G) (H) (J)
15 (A) (B) (C) (D)
16 (F) (G) (H) (J)
17 (A) (B) (C) (D)
18 (F) (G) (H) (J)
19 (A) (B) (C) (D)
20 (F) (G) (H) (J)
21 (A) (B) (C) (D)

Part 2: LANGUAGE EXPRESSION

E1 (A) (B) (C) (D)
1 (A) (B) (C) (D)
2 (F) (G) (H) (J)
3 (A) (B) (C) (D)
4 (F) (G) (H) (J)
5 (A) (B) (C) (D)
6 (F) (G) (H) (J)
7 (A) (B) (C) (D)
8 (F) (G) (H) (J)
9 (A) (B) (C) (D)
10 (F) (G) (H) (J)
11 (A) (B) (C) (D)
12 (F) (G) (H) (J)
13 (A) (B) (C) (D)
14 (F) (G) (H) (J)
15 (A) (B) (C) (D)
16 (F) (G) (H) (J)
17 (A) (B) (C) (D)
18 (F) (G) (H) (J)
19 (A) (B) (C) (D)
20 (F) (G) (H) (J)

Part 3: SPELLING

E1 (A) (B) (C) (D)
E2 (F) (G) (H) (J)
1 (A) (B) (C) (D)
2 (F) (G) (H) (J)
3 (A) (B) (C) (D)
4 (F) (G) (H) (J)
5 (A) (B) (C) (D)
6 (F) (G) (H) (J)
7 (A) (B) (C) (D)
8 (F) (G) (H) (J)
9 (A) (B) (C) (D)
10 (F) (G) (H) (J)
11 (A) (B) (C) (D)
12 (F) (G) (H) (J)
13 (A) (B) (C) (D)
14 (F) (G) (H) (J)
15 (A) (B) (C) (D)
16 (F) (G) (H) (J)
17 (A) (B) (C) (D)
18 (F) (G) (H) (J)
19 (A) (B) (C) (D)
20 (F) (G) (H) (J)

1-57768-976-3 *Spectrum Test Practice 6*

Name _____ Date _____

LANGUAGE PRACTICE TEST

● Part 1: Language Mechanics

Directions: Fill in the circle for the punctuation that is needed in the sentence. Choose "None" if no further punctuation is needed.

Example

E1. "When will we ever get there" asked Nina.

- (A) .
- (B) ?
- (C) !
- (D) None

---

1. I have lived in Flint Grand Rapids, and Philadelphia.
   - (A) :
   - (B) .
   - (C) ,
   - (D) None

2. Lori you need to decide if you want to play soccer.
   - (F) .
   - (G) ;
   - (H) ,
   - (J) None

3. "That was the most fun I've ever had!" exclaimed Frank.
   - (A) ,
   - (B) :
   - (C) "
   - (D) None

4. "Let's play computer games, said Phil.
   - (F) !
   - (G) "
   - (H) ,
   - (J) None

For numbers 5–7 in the next column, read each answer. Fill in the space for the choice that has a punctuation error. If there is no mistake, fill in the fourth answer space.

5.
   - (A) Read the directions carefully
   - (B) Then put the set together
   - (C) one step at a time.
   - (D) No mistakes

6.
   - (F) I can hardly wait
   - (G) to see my friend Sandra.
   - (H) She lives in Alaska.
   - (J) No mistakes

7.
   - (A) Peter says he wants to be a pilot,
   - (B) police officer or park ranger
   - (C) when he grows up.
   - (D) No mistakes

For numbers 8 and 9, read each sentence with a blank. Choose the word or words that best fit(s) in the blank and show(s) the correct punctuation.

8. We will be gone on vacation all next _____ and our neighbor will feed our pets.
   - (F) week
   - (G) week!
   - (H) week,
   - (J) week:

9. _____ my dog's fault that my homework is late.
   - (A) Its
   - (B) It's
   - (C) Its'
   - (D) Its's

GO ON

LANGUAGE PRACTICE TEST

Part 1: Language Mechanics (cont.)

For numbers 10–13, read each group of sentences. Find the one that is written correctly and shows the correct capitalization and punctuation.

10. Ⓕ Shaquila and janelle, love to do challenging word puzzles, together.

    Ⓖ In 1930 my mother was born in Saginaw Michigan.

    Ⓗ Would you like to own a skunk. I would but my mom would not.

    Ⓙ We did experiments in Mr. Newman's class. Dave, our student aide, assisted.

11. Ⓐ In 1923, dad was born to cora and vern in Eastern Michigan.

    Ⓑ Thats Freds' pet frog. Please leave it there.

    Ⓒ Mom and Dad will take us to see our cousins' new home in Columbus.

    Ⓓ We need to go now? Mrs Fairey is waiting.

12. Ⓕ Did you read *wind in the Willows!* Its my favorite book.

    Ⓖ Allie asked, does anyone know where I left jacks coat?"

    Ⓗ "Does anyone know the way to ivy street?" the man inquired.

    Ⓙ She wants to bring her dog Hershey to Ms. Sweet's class.

13. Ⓐ I love french fries, english muffins and german potato salad.

    Ⓑ No, added Abigail, "I will not ride with you"

Ⓒ "Yes," said Rene. "It's a beautiful day today."

Ⓓ My teacher Mr Winters is marrying Miss Summers in june.

For numbers 14–16, read the sentence with a blank. Fill in the circle for the answer choice that fits best in the blank and has correct capitalization and punctuation.

14. **My aunt lives just a few miles from _____.**

    Ⓕ Lake Superior

    Ⓖ lake Superior

    Ⓗ lake, Superior

    Ⓙ lake superior

15. **The bus is _____ we call your mom?**

    Ⓐ late, should

    Ⓑ late? Should

    Ⓒ late should

    Ⓓ late. Should

16. **Maddie found a _____ under her chair.**

    Ⓕ dime, and two nickels,

    Ⓖ Dime and two Nickels,

    Ⓗ dime and two nickels,

    Ⓙ dime and two nickels

Choose the correct answer for number 17.

17. **Which is the correct way to end a letter?**

    Ⓐ Sincerely yours;

    Ⓑ Sincerely yours,

    Ⓒ Sincerely Yours,

    Ⓓ Sincerely, yours,

GO ON

LANGUAGE PRACTICE TEST
Part 1: Language Mechanics (cont.)

Tina is writing a report on John Henry for a class assignment. Read her report and use it to do numbers 18–21.

(1) For more than a <u>century americans</u> have sung about the mighty deeds of John Henry. (2) You have probably heard the ballad, or folk song, about this giant among railroad workers. (3) The song tells of a "steel-driving man" who competed in a contest with a steam drill.

(4) There really was a person named John Henry. (5) He was an <u>African-American</u> railroad construction worker. (6) But, according to most accounts, he died from an accident in a railroad tunnel. (7) Writers generally contend that the race against the steam drill is invented folklore.

(8) Lovers of legends and <u>folk tales however</u> think otherwise. (9) They believe that the duel with the steam drill actually occurred. (10) Some say it took place in <u>west Virginia, in</u> 1870. (11) Others maintain that it happened in Alabama about the year 1882.

18. In sentence 1, <u>century americans</u> is best written —
   (F) century Americans
   (G) Century, Americans
   (H) century, Americans
   (J) As it is

19. In sentence 5, <u>African-American</u> is best written —
   (A) African-american
   (B) African-American,
   (C) african-american
   (D) As it is

20. In sentence 8, <u>folk tales however</u> is best written —
   (F) folk tales, however,
   (G) folk tales however,
   (H) folktales, however
   (J) As it is

21. In sentence 10, <u>west virginia, in</u> is best written —
   (A) West Virginia, in
   (B) West Virginia in
   (C) west Virginia in
   (D) As it is

STOP

LANGUAGE PRACTICE TEST

● Part 2: Language Expression

Directions: For E1, find the underlined part that is the simple predicate of the sentence. Then follow the directions for each part of this test.

Example

E1. My silly dog meows like a cat.
   Ⓐ   Ⓑ   Ⓒ   Ⓓ

For number 1, choose the word or phrase that best completes the sentence.

1.   It has been snowing _____ for more than two days.
   Ⓐ steady
   Ⓑ steadier
   Ⓒ steadily
   Ⓓ steadiest

For number 2, choose the answer that is a complete and correctly written sentence.

2.   Ⓕ Taking a vacation at Disney World during the holiday.
   Ⓖ They are writing to their.
   Ⓗ Because they like roasting marshmallows over campfires.
   Ⓙ Janette's family will be renting a cottage for the entire month of July.

For numbers 3–5, read each answer choice. Fill in the circle for the choice that has a usage error. If there is no mistake, fill in the circle for the fourth answer.

3.   Ⓐ Talisha's mom arrived early and
   Ⓑ didn't give me no time
   Ⓒ to finish my breakfast.
   Ⓓ No mistakes

4.   Ⓕ The boys is writing to
   Ⓖ their congresswoman
   Ⓗ to express their concern.
   Ⓙ No mistakes

5.   Ⓐ The monkeys at the zoo
   Ⓑ enjoy swinging from the branches
   Ⓒ and playing with their keepers.
   Ⓓ No mistakes

For number 6, find the underlined word that is the simple subject of the sentence.

6.   Our local restaurant serves the best
          Ⓕ   Ⓖ   Ⓗ
   spaghetti.
      Ⓙ

For number 7, find the underlined word that is the simple predicate of the sentence.

7.   The amusement park had over two
             Ⓐ   Ⓑ Ⓒ
   million visitors each summer.
              Ⓓ

GO ON

Name _____ Date _____

LANGUAGE PRACTICE TEST
Part 2: Language Expression (cont.)

For numbers 8–10, choose the answer that best combines the underlined sentences.

8. **The chipmunk scampered away.**
   The chipmunk carried an acorn.

   - F The chipmunk scampered away, and it carried an acorn.
   - G The chipmunk carried an acorn, and it scampered away.
   - H The chipmunk scampered away carrying an acorn.
   - J Scampering away, the chipmunk carried an acorn.

9. **Maysel walked to the store.**
   She wanted to buy new shoes.

   - A Maysel walked to the store, and she wanted to buy new shoes.
   - B Wanting to buy new shoes, Maysel walked to the store.
   - C Although Maysel walked to the store, she wanted to buy new shoes.
   - D Maysel walked to the store to buy new shoes.

10. **Kyle is in line.**
    Austin is in line too.
    They are waiting in line to ride the roller coaster.

    - F Waiting in line to ride the roller coaster are Kyle and Austin.
    - G Kyle and Austin are waiting in line to ride the roller coaster.
    - H Kyle is in line and Austin is too to ride the roller coaster.
    - J Kyle is in line to ride the roller coaster and so is Austin.

For numbers 11 and 12, choose the best way of expressing the idea.

11.
    - A I ran in the race, and I came in second, which made my grandfather proud.
    - B I made my grandfather proud when I ran in the race and when I came in second.
    - C When I came in second in the race I ran, my grandfather was proud.
    - D My grandfather was proud when I came in second in the race.

12.
    - F I walked past a pasture to get to school, and there were cows there.
    - G I walked past a cow pasture to get to school.
    - H Cows were in the pasture I walked past to get to school.
    - J I walked to school and passed a pasture with cows in it.

GO ON

Read the paragraph below. Find the best topic sentence for the paragraph.

13. _____. I attached the buttons to a T-shirt and hung it on the wall. When friends and family learned of my collection, everyone started to give me buttons. Now I have so many buttons that I keep them in a large box under my bed.

   (A) Collecting buttons can be expensive.

   (B) My grandma had a button collection when she was small.

   (C) In the beginning, my collection was very small.

   (D) I don't like collecting buttons.

Find the answer choice that best develops the topic sentence.

14. **Making fudge the old-fashioned way is not easy.**

   (F) Most recipes allow you to use a microwave oven.

   (G) Just go the store and pick up a box mix.

   (H) It requires patience and skill, but it can be worth the effort.

   (J) Add butter and vanilla.

Read the paragraph below. Find the sentence that does not belong in the paragraph.

15. **(1) Bones are the super-structure of the human body. (2) They support muscles and organs and give the body its size and shape. (3) Bones grow as a person's body grows. (4) Yellow bone marrow contains fat. (5) They become thicker and stronger. (6) Like other organs, bones require nourishment to remain strong.**

   (A) Sentence 2

   (B) Sentence 3

   (C) Sentence 4

   (D) Sentence 5

Read the paragraph below. Find the sentence that best fits the blank in the paragraph.

16. **Most pictures of Abraham Lincoln that appear in textbooks show him with a beard. _____. It was not until he ran for the presidency in 1860 that he began to grow a beard.**

   (F) Lincoln was born in a log cabin.

   (G) But for most of his political life, Lincoln was clean-shaven.

   (H) His wife, Mary, liked Lincoln with a beard.

   (J) Lincoln was too busy with the war to be concerned with his appearance.

GO ON

LANGUAGE PRACTICE TEST

Part 2: Language Expression (cont.)

Read this story about two brothers. Use it to do numbers 17–20.

(1) Kerry was always wary of his brother: listening for footsteps or watching for flying objects such as books, toys, or sticks. (2) Once it was a large platter of pancakes. (3) Kerry had to keep his eyes open. (4) He also had to keep his ears open at all times.

(5) Although Kerry and Jimmy were only a year apart, the boys were as differenter as Laurel and Hardy or Fred and Barney. (6) Jimmy, the older brother, was in seventh grade and was already six-feet tall and weighed 180 pounds. (7) But his mom loved him and thought he was a good boy. (8) Jimmy was especially frightening today because he had a temper, which was large to match his size.

(9) Today was the day of the annual race competition between the sixth and seventh graders. (10) The sixth graders were sure to win. (11) What Kerry lacked in size, he made up for in speed. (12) He was the fastest runner in the school. (13) And that was the problem. (14) Jimmy would be furious.

17. How are sentences 3 and 4 best combined?

Ⓐ Kerry had to keep his eyes open, and he had to keep his ears open at all times.

Ⓑ At all times, Kerry had to keep open his eyes and his ears also.

Ⓒ Kerry at all times had to keep his eyes open and his ears also.

Ⓓ Kerry had to keep his eyes and ears open at all times.

18. Which sentence does not belong in this story?

Ⓕ Sentence 2

Ⓖ Sentence 7

Ⓗ Sentence 8

Ⓙ Sentence 14

19. How is sentence 8 best written?

Ⓐ Jimmy had a temper to match his size, which made him especially frightening today.

Ⓑ Like his large size, Jimmy's temper was also large today, which made him especially frightening.

Ⓒ Jimmy had a large temper and a large size, which made him especially frightening today.

Ⓓ Today Jimmy had a temper, which was large to match his size, and he was especially frightening.

20. In sentence 5, how is <u>were as differenter as</u> best written?

Ⓕ were different as

Ⓖ were as different as

Ⓗ were differently as

Ⓙ As it is

LANGUAGE PRACTICE TEST

● Part 3: Spelling

Directions: For E1, mark the word that is spelled correctly and fits best in the blank. For E2, look for the underlined word that has a spelling mistake. Fill in your answer. Then follow the directions for each part of this test.

Examples

E1. No matter the _____, try to be positive.
- (A) sercumstances
- (B) circumstances
- (C) cercumstenses
- (D) circomstances

E2.
- (F) breakfast <u>nook</u>
- (G) sing in <u>unison</u>
- (H) <u>saffire</u> ring
- (J) call a <u>truce</u>

For numbers 1–6, find the word that is spelled correctly and fits best in the blank.

1. She was in _____.
- (A) anguish
- (B) angish
- (C) enguish
- (D) anguishe

2. Please take out the _____.
- (F) garbage
- (G) gerbage
- (H) garbagge
- (J) gharbage

3. Stop talking _____!
- (A) nonsence
- (B) nonsense
- (C) nonsince
- (D) noncence

4. Don't _____.
- (F) exaggerate
- (G) exagerate
- (H) ecagerate
- (J) excagerate

5. This is an _____ time.
- (A) enconvenient
- (B) incunvient
- (C) inconvenient
- (D) encunvenient

6. Send a _____ greeting.
- (F) courdial
- (G) corgial
- (H) cordial
- (J) courgial

For numbers 7–10, read the phrases. Choose the phrase in which the underlined word is not spelled correctly.

7.
- (A) <u>flourescent</u> light
- (B) garden <u>hose</u>
- (C) one <u>fortnight</u>
- (D) physical <u>characteristics</u>

8.
- (F) northern <u>hemisphere</u>
- (G) sincere <u>congradulations</u>
- (H) <u>impart</u> wisdom
- (J) 2000 <u>census</u>

9.
- (A) condensed <u>version</u>
- (B) the dog <u>yelped</u>
- (C) <u>quench</u> your thirst
- (D) midnight <u>rade</u>

10.
- (F) <u>razer</u> blade
- (G) <u>gorgeous</u> dress
- (H) blue <u>lagoon</u>
- (J) swift <u>gazelle</u>

GO ON

LANGUAGE PRACTICE TEST
Part 3: Spelling (cont.)

For numbers 11–13, read each answer. Fill in the space for the choice that has a spelling error. If there is no mistake, fill in the circle for the last answer.

11.   Ⓐ   molecule
       Ⓑ   pavillion
       Ⓒ   oath
       Ⓓ   No mistakes

12.   Ⓕ   nominate
       Ⓖ   tournament
       Ⓗ   tradgedy
       Ⓙ   No mistakes

13.   Ⓐ   vigerous
       Ⓑ   revolution
       Ⓒ   gourd
       Ⓓ   No mistakes

For numbers 14–16, read each phrase. One of the underlined words is not spelled correctly for the way it is used in the phrase. Fill in the circle for the word that is not spelled correctly.

14.   Ⓕ   fix the <u>leek</u>
       Ⓖ   change the <u>topic</u>
       Ⓗ   pay a <u>toll</u>
       Ⓙ   <u>scant</u> clothing

15.   Ⓐ   garbage <u>heap</u>
       Ⓑ   <u>roe</u> the boat
       Ⓒ   <u>loaf</u> of bread
       Ⓓ   tie the <u>knot</u>

16.   Ⓕ   a <u>holy</u> man
       Ⓖ   run an <u>errand</u>
       Ⓗ   weather <u>vein</u>
       Ⓙ   <u>sole</u> survivor

For numbers 17–20, find the underlined part that is misspelled. If all of the words are spelled correctly, fill in the circle for <u>No mistake</u>.

17.   It is <u>awful</u> to <u>experience</u> an <u>earthquake</u>.
      Ⓐ   Ⓑ   Ⓒ
     <u>No mistake.</u>
      Ⓓ

18.   <u>Parakeats</u> can <u>mimic</u> many <u>phrases</u>.
        Ⓕ   Ⓖ   Ⓗ
     <u>No mistake.</u>
      Ⓙ

19.   As a <u>neccessary</u> <u>precaution</u>, we
          Ⓐ   Ⓑ
     <u>recommend</u> that you stay seated.
       Ⓒ
     <u>No mistake.</u>
      Ⓓ

20.   We <u>picnicked</u> in a <u>passture</u> overlooking a
          Ⓕ   Ⓖ
     <u>quaint</u> little <u>village</u>. <u>No mistake.</u>
      Ⓗ   Ⓙ

STOP

LANGUAGE PRACTICE TEST

● Part 4: Study Skills

Directions: Follow the directions given. Fill in the circle for the answer of your choice.

Example

Outline

Mammals
1. Rodents
2. _____
3. Primates
4. Canines
5. Felines

E1. Which of these would fit best in line 2 of the outline on the left?

- Ⓐ Mice
- Ⓑ Marsupials
- Ⓒ Cats
- Ⓓ Amphibians

Study the newspaper below. Use it to do numbers 1–4.

Monday, June 3

DAILY SENTINEL

Today's Weather— Sunny, high 82

INDEX

Business C1
Classified B6
Comics A20
Crosswords A19
Editorials A12
Sports D1
Television A21
The Region B1
Weather B14
World News A2

Firefighter Rescues Boy

This morning at 4:00 A.M., a fire erupted in a private residence located at 3345 Palmer Street. The family dog woke the family from their slumber with its insistent barking. All but the youngest son were able to escape from the home. Firefighters were on the scene within minutes after a neighbor alerted them.

(Photo on page A5)

In a daring move, a firefighter was able to rescue the young boy by
(Continued on page A5)

Local Business Volunteers Aid

After the recent earthquake that left thousands homeless, a local business temporarily shut its doors and bused its employees to the scene of the devastation. The employees set up tents to serve hot meals and dispense food and clothing. Ron Wardie, owner of Supply Co., told reporters, "It was my employees' idea. I was reluctant at first. But they were so willing to donate their time, I couldn't help but say yes."

(Continued on page A6)

1. How many sections does this paper have?
- Ⓐ 1
- Ⓑ 2
- Ⓒ 3
- Ⓓ 4

2. Which of these appears on A5?
- Ⓕ Weather
- Ⓖ The continuation of the story about the firefighter
- Ⓗ World News
- Ⓙ The continuation of the story about the local business

3. What was the weather on the day this newspaper was published?
- Ⓐ Cloudy with a high of 72
- Ⓑ The weather is listed on D1.
- Ⓒ Sunny with a high of 82
- Ⓓ It can't be determined.

4. In which section would you be most likely to find job listings?
- Ⓕ A
- Ⓖ B
- Ⓗ C
- Ⓙ D

GO ON

LANGUAGE PRACTICE TEST
Part 4: Study Skills (cont.)

Matthew is writing a report about baboons in the wild. Keep this purpose in mind when you do numbers 5 and 6.

5. **Matthew used the book titled *Baboons and Other Primates*. Where in the book should Matthew look to find the definition of the word *bipedal*?**

    (A) the index
    (B) the glossary
    (C) the table of contents
    (D) the introduction

6. **Which of these should Matthew include in his report?**

    (F) the habitat and diet of baboons
    (G) the location of zoos that feature baboons
    (H) baboons as pets
    (J) information on chimpanzees

For number 7, read the sentences. Then choose the key words Matthew should include in his notes on baboons.

7.   Baboons live in social groups presided over by one dominant male. During the day, the group forages for food. At night, the baboons sleep in rocky outcrops or in trees. Their diet consists mostly of grass seeds, roots, bulbs, and other plant parts. When available, they will also eat insects and small animals. Baboons sometimes live in harsh environments with little water. If needed, they may dig to find it.

    (A) dig in rocky outcrops
    (B) dominant females
    (C) prefer to eat small animals
    (D) forage for food and water

Study this dictionary entry. Then do numbers 8–10.

> ex•haust (ĭg-zôst´) *Verb.* **-hausted**, **-hausting**. 1. To wear out completely. 2. To drain of resources or properties; deplete. 3. To treat completely; cover thoroughly: *exhaust a topic.* —*Noun.* 4. The escape or release of vaporous waste material, as from an engine. 5. A duct or pipe through which waste material is emitted.

8. **Which definition of the word *exhaust* is used in this sentence?**

    The car's exhaust gave Marjorie a stomachache.

    (F) Definition 2
    (G) Definition 3
    (H) Definition 4
    (J) Definition 5

9. **Which definition of the word *exhaust* means "to cover entirely"?**

    (A) Definition 1
    (B) Definition 2
    (C) Definition 3
    (D) Definition 4

10. **Which of these could be guidewords on a dictionary page that includes the word *exhaust*?**

    (F) exert/exit
    (G) exhort/exist
    (H) exclude/exercise
    (J) exhibit/expect

Name _____   Date _____

MATH: CONCEPTS

● Lesson 1: Numeration

Directions: Read and work each problem. Find the correct answer. Fill in the circle for your choice.

Examples

A. Which group of numbers is ordered from greatest to least?

- Ⓐ 7,834 1,979 7,878 3,876
- Ⓑ 1,234 3,456 5,689 7,893
- Ⓒ 3,456 4,576 4,579 5,423
- Ⓓ 8,778 6,545 2,324 1,645

B. Which of these is the expanded numeral for 9,804?

- Ⓕ 9,000 + 800 + 40
- Ⓖ 9,000 + 800 + 10 + 4
- Ⓗ 9,000 + 800 + 4
- Ⓙ 9 + 8 + 0 + 4

 Clue Read the problem carefully and look at all answer choices before you mark the one you think is correct.

● Practice

1. $\sqrt{25}$
   - Ⓐ 7
   - Ⓑ 5
   - Ⓒ 4
   - Ⓓ 6

2. What is the greatest common factor of 16 and 64?
   - Ⓕ 4
   - Ⓖ 8
   - Ⓗ 16
   - Ⓙ 2

3. Which of these is a multiple of 13?
   - Ⓐ 169
   - Ⓑ 196
   - Ⓒ 133
   - Ⓓ 159

4. What number is expressed by (8 x 10,000) + (5 x 1,000) + (3 x 100) + (8 x 1)?
   - Ⓕ 805,308
   - Ⓖ 85,308
   - Ⓗ 850,308
   - Ⓙ 805,380

5. Which of these numbers is between 5,945,089 and 5,956,108?
   - Ⓐ 5,995,098
   - Ⓑ 5,943,787
   - Ⓒ 5,947,109
   - Ⓓ 5,549,090

6. Which of these is another way to write 7 x 7 x 7 x 7 x 7?
   - Ⓕ 5^7
   - Ⓖ 7^5
   - Ⓗ 7 x 5
   - Ⓙ 7 + 5

GO ON

MATH: CONCEPTS

● **Lesson 1: Numeration (cont.)**

7. **Which numeral comes right after XII?**
   - (A) XIII
   - (B) XIV
   - (C) XV
   - (D) XX

8. **An employee in a warehouse has 84 games to pack into boxes. Each box can hold 18 games. How many boxes will the employee need for all the games?**
   - (F) 6
   - (G) 4
   - (H) 5
   - (J) 8

9. **At her party, Emily wants to serve each of her friends a hotdog and a bun. There are 8 hotdogs in a package but only 6 buns in a bag. What is the least amount of hotdogs Emily must buy so that she has the same amount of hotdogs and buns?**
   - (A) 48
   - (B) 16
   - (C) 8
   - (D) 24

10. **The expanded number for 64,090 is —**
    - (F) $6 + 4 + 0 + 9 + 0$
    - (G) $(64 \times 10,000) + 900$
    - (H) $(6 \times 10,000) + (4 \times 1,000) + (9 \times 10)$
    - (J) $(6 \times 1,000) + (4 \times 1,000) + (9 \times 10)$

11. **What are all the factors of 16?**
    - (A) 2 and 4
    - (B) 2, 4, and 8
    - (C) 32, 48, and 64
    - (D) 1, 2, 4, 8, and 16

12. **What is the smallest number that can be divided evenly by 5 and 45?**
    - (F) 135
    - (G) 225
    - (H) 90
    - (J) 125

13. **What is the greatest common factor of 42 and 54?**
    - (A) 6
    - (B) 7
    - (C) 4
    - (D) 9

14. **Which number is less than 176 and more than 165?**
    - (F) 177
    - (G) 164
    - (H) 167
    - (J) 154

15. **7 millions, 8 thousands, 3 tens, and 7 ones =**
    - (A) 780,037
    - (B) 7,080,037
    - (C) 7,008,037
    - (D) 708,307

16. **196 =**
    - (F) 14^2
    - (G) 8^3
    - (H) 16^2
    - (J) 6^3

STOP

MATH: CONCEPTS

● Lesson 2: Number Concepts

Directions: Read and work each problem. Find the correct answer. Mark the space for your choice.

Examples

A. eighty-nine =

- (A) 98
- (B) 89
- (C) 809
- (D) 88

B. The 7 in 68,743 means —

- (F) 7,000
- (G) 700
- (H) 70
- (J) 7

Look for key words and numbers that will help you find the answers. Remember, you might not have to compute to find the correct answer to a problem. If a problem is too difficult, skip it and come back to it later.

● Practice

1. What number is 2,000 less than 765,422?
   - (A) 565,422
   - (B) 765,222
   - (C) 763,422
   - (D) 745,422

2. Which expression shows 50 as a multiple of prime numbers?
   - (F) 25 x 2
   - (G) 2 x 5 x 5
   - (H) 50 x 1
   - (J) 10 x 5

3. How many even numbers are there between 4 and 24?
   - (A) 6
   - (B) 8
   - (C) 12
   - (D) 9

4. A number is less than 443 and greater than 397. The sum of the ones digit and the tens digit in the number is 5. The ones digit is 3. What is the number?
   - (F) 423
   - (G) 432
   - (H) 323
   - (J) 322

5. What number is missing from the pattern shown below?

   | 2, 6, 14, ___, 62, 126 |

   - (A) 18
   - (B) 22
   - (C) 30
   - (D) 28

GO ON

MATH: CONCEPTS

● Lesson 2: Number Concepts (cont.)

6. Which of these numbers has a 5 in the tens place?
   - (F) 4,568
   - (G) 5,395
   - (H) 8,456
   - (J) 7,675

7. Thirty thousand, six =
   - (A) 36,000
   - (B) 30,600
   - (C) 306,000
   - (D) 30,006

8. Which of these is a prime number?
   - (F) 6
   - (G) 47
   - (H) 39
   - (J) 8

9. How much would the value of 456,881 be decreased by replacing the 6 with a 5?
   - (A) 10,000
   - (B) 1,000
   - (C) 1
   - (D) 100

10. 5,078,093 is read —
    - (F) five hundred seven million, eight thousand, ninety-three
    - (G) five million, seventy-eight thousand, ninety-three
    - (H) five million seventy-eight, ninety-three
    - (J) five hundred seventy-eight million, ninety-three

11. Which of these is a composite number?
    - (A) 27
    - (B) 11
    - (C) 29
    - (D) 51

12. Which numeral has a 6 in both the ten thousands and ones places?
    - (F) 609,546
    - (G) 65,767
    - (H) 59,676
    - (J) 60,386

13. What is the value of 3 in 9.231?
    - (A) 3 tenths
    - (B) 3 tens
    - (C) 3 hundredths
    - (D) 3 thousandths

14. Which group contains both odd and even numbers?
    - (F) 76, 94, 54, 32, 22
    - (G) 33, 51, 11, 99, 37
    - (H) 72, 44, 68, 94, 26
    - (J) 55, 38, 21, 88, 33

15. A number has a 7 in the tens place, a 5 in the ones place, and a 3 in the thousands place. Which number is it?
    - (A) 753
    - (B) 375
    - (C) 7,385
    - (D) 3,175

STOP

MATH: CONCEPTS

● Lesson 3: Properties

Directions: Read and work each problem. Find the correct answer. Mark the space for your choice.

Examples

A. Which is another name for 730 x 1,000?

- Ⓐ 73 x 10,000
- Ⓑ 7300 x 1,000
- Ⓒ 730 x 100
- Ⓓ 70 x 3,000

B. What is 344 rounded to the nearest hundred?

- Ⓕ 350
- Ⓖ 340
- Ⓗ 300
- Ⓙ 400

 Clue Take your best guess when you are unsure of the answer. When you work on scratch paper, be sure to transfer numbers accurately and compute carefully.

● Practice

1. $\dfrac{3}{\square} = \dfrac{18}{36}$

    $\square =$

    - Ⓐ 5
    - Ⓑ 6
    - Ⓒ 8
    - Ⓓ 4

2. Which is another name for 55?

    - Ⓕ (5 x 5) + 10
    - Ⓖ 5 + (5 x 1)
    - Ⓗ 61 − (2 x 3)
    - Ⓙ (3 x 3) x 6

3. The product of 396 x 32.89 is closest to —

    - Ⓐ 900
    - Ⓑ 9,000
    - Ⓒ 13,000
    - Ⓓ 90

4. What number goes in the box to make the number sentence true?

    $$\square > {}^-7$$

    - Ⓕ ⁻15
    - Ⓖ ⁻1
    - Ⓗ ⁻8
    - Ⓙ ⁻9

5. Which of these statements is true?

    - Ⓐ When a whole number is multiplied by 3, the product will always be an odd number.
    - Ⓑ When a whole number is multiplied by 4, the product will always be an even number.
    - Ⓒ All numbers that can be divided by 5 are odd numbers.
    - Ⓓ The product of an odd and even number is always an odd number.

GO ON

MATH: CONCEPTS

● Lesson 3: Properties (cont.)

6. Which number completes the number sentence below?

$7 \times (2 + 5) = \square + 23$

- (F) 11
- (G) 24
- (H) 26
- (J) 13

7. There are 52 weeks in a year. Wilma works 46 weeks each year. During each week, she works 32 hours. Which number sentence below shows how many hours Wilma works in a year?

- (A) $52 \times 32 = \square$
- (B) $46 \times 32 = \square$
- (C) $32 \times 52 = \square$
- (D) $(52 - 46) \times 32 = \square$

8. Which of the tables follows the rule shown below?

Rule: Add 3 to the number in column A, and then multiply by 8 to get the number in column B.

A	B
3	49
4	55
5	61
6	67

(F)

A	B
3	14
4	15
5	16
6	17

(G)

A	B
3	48
4	56
5	64
6	72

(H)

A	B
3	46
4	54
5	62
6	70

(J)

9. A number rounded to the nearest hundred is 98,400. The same number rounded to the nearest thousand is 98,000. Which of these could be the number?

- (A) 98,567
- (B) 98,398p
- (C) 99,123
- (D) 98,745

10. In which of the situations below would you probably use an estimate?

- (F) You owe your sister some money and need to pay her back.
- (G) You are giving a report and want to tell how many ants live in a colony.
- (H) You are responsible for counting the votes in a class election.
- (J) You are the manager of a baseball team and are calculating the batting averages for the players on your team.

11. You helped your mom plant 40 tulip bulbs in the fall. In the spring, 10 of the tulips did not come up at all, and $\frac{1}{3}$ of the rest had yellow flowers. Which of the number sentences below show how to find the number of tulips that had yellow flowers?

- (A) $40 - 10 = \frac{1}{3} \times \square$
- (B) $\frac{1}{3} \times (40 - 10) = \square$
- (C) $(\frac{1}{3} \times 40) - 10 = \square$
- (D) $(\frac{1}{3} \times 10) = \square$

STOP

MATH: CONCEPTS

● Lesson 4: Fractions and Decimals

Directions: Read and work each problem. Find the correct answer. Mark the space for your choice.

Example

A. How much of the figure below is shaded?

- (A) $\frac{1}{3}$
- (B) $\frac{1}{8}$
- (C) $\frac{1}{2}$
- (D) $\frac{1}{4}$

Clue: Pay close attention to the numbers in the problem and in the answer choices. If you misread even one number, you will probably choose the wrong answer. Eliminate answer choices you know are wrong.

● Practice

1. Which of these is six hundredths?
   - (A) 0.006
   - (B) 0.060
   - (C) 0.600
   - (D) 6.100

2. $\frac{54}{1000}$
   - (F) 5.400
   - (G) 0.5400
   - (H) 0.054
   - (J) 0.54

3. Which of these is greater than $\frac{3}{5}$?
   - (A) 1/4
   - (B) 1/2
   - (C) 7/8
   - (D) 1/3

4. On the number line below, which arrow points most closely to 2.8?

   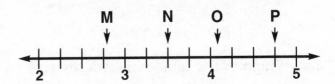

   - (F) M
   - (G) N
   - (H) O
   - (J) P

5. Which of these is between 0.07 and 0.5 in value?
   - (A) 0.18
   - (B) 0.81
   - (C) 0.007
   - (D) 0.018

GO ON

Name _____   Date_____

MATH: CONCEPTS

● **Lesson 4: Fractions and Decimals (cont.)**

6. The length of $\overline{ST}$ is what fraction of $\overline{UV}$?

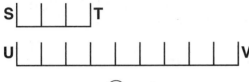

- (F) $\frac{1}{6}$
- (G) $\frac{1}{3}$
- (H) $\frac{2}{3}$
- (J) $\frac{1}{5}$

7. What is the least common denominator for $\frac{1}{3}$, $\frac{3}{5}$, and $\frac{1}{2}$?

- (A) 15
- (B) 30
- (C) 45
- (D) 60

8. Which decimal is another name for $\frac{5}{1,000}$?

- (F) 0.005
- (G) 5
- (H) 0.050
- (J) 0.5000

9. Which group of decimals is ordered from greatest to least?

- (A) 3.021 4.123 0.788 1.234
- (B) 0.567 0.870 0.912 1.087
- (C) 2.067 1.989 1.320 0.879
- (D) 0.003 1.076 0.873 0.002

10. Which of these numbers can go in the box to make the number sentence true ?

$$\frac{1}{\square} > \frac{1}{4}$$

- (F) 3
- (G) 5
- (H) 6
- (J) 7

11. Which fraction is another name for $3\frac{2}{5}$?

- (A) $\frac{6}{5}$
- (B) $\frac{11}{5}$
- (C) $\frac{37}{5}$
- (D) $\frac{17}{5}$

12. Which fraction is in its simplest form?

- (F) $\frac{5}{10}$
- (G) $\frac{3}{7}$
- (H) $\frac{3}{9}$
- (J) $\frac{7}{42}$

13. Which of the decimals below is thirty-two and thirteen hundredths?

- (A) 3,213
- (B) 32.13
- (C) 32.013
- (D) 3,200.13

STOP

Name _____   Date _____

SAMPLE TEST

● **Directions:** Read each question. Find the correct answer. Mark the space for your choice.

Examples

E1. Which of these groups of numbers is in order from least to greatest?

Ⓐ 16,089 14,876 18,999 22,800
Ⓑ 22,888 22,989 22,897 23,001
Ⓒ 12,954 13,656 13,875 15,877
Ⓓ 12,443 11,339 11,123 10,458

E2. What is 7,453 rounded to the nearest hundred?

Ⓕ 7,500
Ⓖ 7,400
Ⓗ 7,000
Ⓙ 7,450

1. Which digit means ten thousands in the numeral 5,873,096?

Ⓐ 8
Ⓑ 3
Ⓒ 7
Ⓓ 0

2. Which of these numbers best shows what part of the bar is shaded?

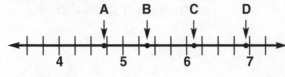

Ⓕ $\frac{1}{4}$

Ⓖ 0.7

Ⓗ $\frac{1}{3}$

Ⓙ 0.5

3. Which letter marks $4\frac{6}{10}$ on this number line?

A   B   C   D

4   5   6   7

Ⓐ A
Ⓑ B
Ⓒ C
Ⓓ D

4. 7,768 ÷ 17 is between —

Ⓕ 300 and 400
Ⓖ 600 and 700
Ⓗ 450 and 550
Ⓙ 250 and 350

5. Which of these is a composite number?

Ⓐ 13
Ⓑ 31
Ⓒ 57
Ⓓ 15

6. In a book, which chapter comes right after chapter IX?

Ⓕ XI
Ⓖ X
Ⓗ XII
Ⓙ XIV

7. Which of these is another way to write 606,344?

Ⓐ 60 + 63 + 44
Ⓑ 60,000 + 6,000 + 300 + 40 + 4
Ⓒ 600,000 + 6,000 + 300 + 40 + 4
Ⓓ 600,000 + 60,000 + 300 + 40 + 4

GO ON

Name _____ Date _____

8. What number is missing from the pattern below?

$\frac{4}{10}$, 0.5, $\frac{6}{10}$, 0.7, __, 0.9

(F) $\frac{8}{10}$

(G) $\frac{7}{10}$

(H) 0.8

(J) 0.08

9. Pam had 45 packages of licorice and wanted to put them in bags that could hold 10 packages each. How many bags could she fill completely?

(A) 5
(B) 4
(C) 6
(D) 2

10. Which of these symbols goes in the box to make this number sentence true?

$\frac{8}{10} + \frac{2}{4}$ □ 2

(F) =
(G) >
(H) <
(J) >

11. What is 0.465 rounded to the nearest tenth?

(A) 0.5
(B) 0.7
(C) 0.6
(D) 0.05

12. $\sqrt{36}$

(F) 12
(G) 3
(H) 6
(J) 360

13. Which number is three hundred nine thousand, five hundred fifty-eight?

(A) 3,090,558
(B) 309,508
(C) 309,558
(D) 3,009,558

14. What number completes this number sentence?

4 x 35 = 4 x (□ + 5)

(F) 35
(G) 30
(H) 3
(J) 38

15. Using the digits 8, 4, 7, and 6, which of the following are the smallest and the largest decimal numbers you can write?

(A) 0.8476 and 0.6748
(B) 0.8746 and 0.4678
(C) 0.4678 and 0.8764
(D) 0.6748 and 0.8674

STOP

MATH: COMPUTATION

● Lesson 5: Whole Numbers (All Operations)

Directions: Read and work each problem. Be sure that you are performing the called for operation. Fill in the circle for your choice.

Examples

A.
$$4,988$$
$$+ \ 8,765$$

- Ⓐ 12,753
- Ⓑ 13,853
- Ⓒ 13,753
- Ⓓ None of these

B. 456 + 768 + 654 =

- Ⓕ 1,569
- Ⓖ 2,468
- Ⓗ 1,468
- Ⓙ None of these

 Clue

If the answer you find is not one of the answer choices, rework the problem on scratch paper. If you rework a problem and still find that the right number is not given, mark the choice for "None of these."

● Practice

1.
$$678$$
$$1,234$$
$$+ \ 679$$

- Ⓐ 2,491
- Ⓑ 1,591
- Ⓒ 2,591
- Ⓓ None of these

5.
$$45,676$$
$$+ \ 78,543$$

- Ⓐ 124,219
- Ⓑ 115,219
- Ⓒ 134,129
- Ⓓ None of these

2. 6,789 ÷ 13 =

- Ⓕ 522R3
- Ⓖ 521R7
- Ⓗ 52R3
- Ⓙ None of these

6. 24)‾6,998

- Ⓕ 292R11
- Ⓖ 291R14
- Ⓗ 392R7
- Ⓙ None of these

3. 756 x 432 =

- Ⓐ 236,592
- Ⓑ 326,592
- Ⓒ 336,592
- Ⓓ None of these

7. 812 x 789 =

- Ⓐ 1,640,668
- Ⓑ 560,668
- Ⓒ 640,668
- Ⓓ None of these

4.
$$123,489$$
$$- \ 79,654$$

- Ⓕ 42,835
- Ⓖ 93,143
- Ⓗ 43,834
- Ⓙ None of these

8.
$$45,678$$
$$123,602$$
$$+ \ 345,999$$

- Ⓕ 525,279
- Ⓖ 815,279
- Ⓗ 515,278
- Ⓙ None of these

STOP

Name _____   Date _____

MATH: COMPUTATION

● Lesson 6: Addition and Subtraction of Fractions

Directions: Fill in the circle for the correct answer to each addition and subtraction problem. Choose NG if the right answer is not given.

Examples

A. $\frac{7}{10} + \frac{8}{10} =$

Ⓐ $1\frac{7}{10}$

Ⓑ $\frac{10}{18}$

Ⓒ $1\frac{4}{5}$

Ⓓ NG

B. $\frac{8}{10}$
        $-\frac{5}{10}$

Ⓕ $1\frac{3}{10}$

Ⓖ $\frac{3}{10}$

Ⓗ $\frac{1}{5}$

Ⓙ NG

Clue If the right answer is not given, mark the space for NG, which means "not given."

● Practice

1. $\frac{5}{6} + \frac{1}{12} + \frac{1}{3} =$

Ⓐ $\frac{7}{3}$

Ⓑ $1\frac{1}{4}$

Ⓒ $\frac{11}{12}$

Ⓓ NG

2. $20\frac{2}{5} + 5\frac{5}{6} =$

Ⓕ $26\frac{7}{30}$

Ⓖ $25\frac{7}{12}$

Ⓗ $36\frac{3}{10}$

Ⓙ NG

3. $4\frac{2}{10}$
        $-3\frac{4}{5}$

Ⓐ $1\frac{4}{10}$

Ⓑ $\frac{2}{5}$

Ⓒ $\frac{2}{8}$

Ⓓ NG

4. $12\frac{2}{3} - 9\frac{5}{6} =$

Ⓕ $2\frac{2}{3}$

Ⓖ $22\frac{1}{2}$

Ⓗ $2\frac{5}{6}$

Ⓙ NG

5. $18\frac{3}{4}$
        $+13\frac{5}{8}$

Ⓐ $33\frac{5}{8}$

Ⓑ $5\frac{1}{8}$

Ⓒ $32\frac{3}{8}$

Ⓓ NG

6. $8\frac{1}{3} - 6\frac{5}{6} =$

Ⓕ $1\frac{1}{3}$

Ⓖ $2\frac{1}{6}$

Ⓗ $15\frac{1}{6}$

Ⓙ NG

7. $1\frac{4}{5} + 6\frac{2}{3} =$

Ⓐ $7\frac{1}{3}$

Ⓑ $8\frac{2}{15}$

Ⓒ $5\frac{7}{15}$

Ⓓ NG

8. $12\frac{1}{2}$
        $-7\frac{3}{4}$

Ⓕ $3\frac{3}{4}$

Ⓖ $4\frac{3}{4}$

Ⓗ $20\frac{1}{4}$

Ⓙ NG

STOP

Name _____ Date _____

MATH: COMPUTATION

● Lesson 7: Multiplication of Fractions

Directions: Fill in the circle for the correct answer to each multiplication problem. Choose NG if the right answer is not given.

Examples

A.

$7 \times \frac{1}{9} =$

Ⓐ 63

Ⓑ $\frac{7}{9}$

Ⓒ $7\frac{1}{9}$

Ⓓ NG

B.

$\frac{2}{5} \times 4 =$

Ⓕ $1\frac{3}{5}$

Ⓖ 10

Ⓗ $1\frac{4}{5}$

Ⓙ NG

 Clue If the right answer is not given, mark the space for NG, which means "not given."

● Practice

1.

$\frac{5}{8} \times \frac{4}{15} =$

Ⓐ $\frac{2}{15}$

Ⓑ $\frac{1}{6}$

Ⓒ $\frac{1}{3}$

Ⓓ NG

2.

$1\frac{2}{3}$

$\times 5$

Ⓕ $2\frac{3}{5}$

Ⓖ $8\frac{1}{3}$

Ⓗ $5\frac{2}{3}$

Ⓙ NG

3.

$\frac{7}{12} \times \frac{3}{12} =$

Ⓐ $\frac{3}{24}$

Ⓑ $\frac{3}{48}$

Ⓒ $\frac{21}{44}$

Ⓓ NG

4.

$12 \times \frac{4}{5} =$

Ⓕ $9\frac{2}{8}$

Ⓖ $8\frac{2}{5}$

Ⓗ $9\frac{4}{5}$

Ⓙ NG

5.

$\frac{2}{9}$

$\times \quad \frac{7}{8}$

Ⓐ $\frac{7}{36}$

Ⓑ $\frac{16}{63}$

Ⓒ $\frac{7}{9}$

Ⓓ NG

6.

$\frac{4}{5} \times 11 =$

Ⓕ $7\frac{3}{5}$

Ⓖ $8\frac{4}{5}$

Ⓗ $12\frac{3}{8}$

Ⓙ NG

7.

$\frac{7}{3} \times \frac{6}{9} =$

Ⓐ $\frac{2}{27}$

Ⓑ $\frac{1}{9}$

Ⓒ $1\frac{5}{9}$

Ⓓ NG

8.

$1\frac{1}{12} \times \frac{3}{8} =$

Ⓕ $\frac{31}{32}$

Ⓖ $\frac{1}{4}$

Ⓗ $\frac{3}{32}$

Ⓙ NG

STOP

1-57768-976-3 Spectrum Test Practice 6

Name _____   Date_____

MATH: COMPUTATION

● Lesson 8: Division of Fractions

Directions: Fill in the circle for the correct answer to each division problem. Choose NG if the right answer is not given.

Examples

A.
$\frac{1}{7} \div 6 =$

- (A) 42
- (B) $\frac{1}{42}$
- (C) $\frac{1}{23}$
- (D) NG

B.
$\frac{2}{3} \div \frac{7}{8} =$

- (F) $\frac{7}{12}$
- (G) $\frac{16}{21}$
- (H) $\frac{2}{3}$
- (J) NG

 Clue Pay close attention when dividing fractions. It is easy to make a mistake by forgetting to invert fractions.

● Practice

1.
$\frac{7}{12} \div \frac{3}{4} =$

- (A) $\frac{21}{48}$
- (B) $\frac{1}{3}$
- (C) $\frac{7}{9}$
- (D) NG

2.
$\frac{5}{6} \div \frac{5}{18} =$

- (F) 3
- (G) $\frac{1}{3}$
- (H) $\frac{5}{9}$
- (J) NG

3.
$5 \div \frac{7}{9} =$

- (A) $7\frac{3}{7}$
- (B) $3\frac{6}{7}$
- (C) 8
- (D) NG

4.
$\frac{3}{20} \div \frac{9}{10} =$

- (F) $\frac{1}{6}$
- (G) $\frac{2}{9}$
- (H) $1\frac{2}{7}$
- (J) NG

5.
$2\frac{1}{10} \div 8\frac{2}{5} =$

- (A) $\frac{1}{10}$
- (B) $\frac{1}{4}$
- (C) $\frac{1}{9}$
- (D) NG

6.
$7\frac{1}{2} \div 5\frac{5}{8} =$

- (F) $1\frac{1}{3}$
- (G) $2\frac{2}{5}$
- (H) $1\frac{3}{8}$
- (J) NG

7.
$\frac{8}{9} \div \frac{1}{4} =$

- (A) $5\frac{1}{3}$
- (B) $\frac{1}{36}$
- (C) $3\frac{5}{9}$
- (D) NG

8.
$1\frac{11}{15} \div 1\frac{19}{20} =$

- (F) $\frac{3}{5}$
- (G) $\frac{8}{9}$
- (H) $\frac{1}{7}$
- (J) NG

STOP

MATH: COMPUTATION

● Lesson 9: Addition and Subtraction of Decimals

Directions: Fill in the circle for the correct answer to each problem. Choose NG if the right answer is not given.

Examples

A.

$0.4567 + 0.2369 =$

- (A) 0.6723
- (B) 0.8693
- (C) 0.6936
- (D) NG

B.   2.873
      − 0.620

- (F) 1.253
- (G) 0.654
- (H) 2.253
- (J) NG

If the answer you find is not one of the answer choices, rework the problem on scratch paper. If you still find that the answer is not given, mark the space for NG.

● Practice

1.

$0.4509 + 0.768 =$

- (A) 1.289
- (B) 2.783
- (C) 0.1289
- (D) NG

2.   1.871
      + 0.554

- (F) 1.995
- (G) 0.347
- (H) 2.425
- (J) NG

3.

$3.945 − 1.774 =$

- (A) 0.334
- (B) 2.167
- (C) 2.992
- (D) NG

4.   0.0456
      + 1.847

- (F) 2.964
- (G) 5.935
- (H) 1.8926
- (J) NG

5.

$7.302 + 6.0073 =$

- (A) 13.9033
- (B) 14.3093
- (C) 1.3309
- (D) NG

6.   3.338
      − 1.774

- (F) 1.564
- (G) 15.64
- (H) 0.1564
- (J) NG

7.

$0.0887 + 0.5534 =$

- (A) 0.0642
- (B) 0.6421
- (C) 1.6421
- (D) NG

8.   0.9876
      − 0.8523

- (F) 0.076
- (G) 0.1353
- (H) 0.01353
- (J) NG

STOP

MATH: COMPUTATION

● Lesson 10: Multiplication of Decimals

Directions: Fill in the circle for the correct answer to each problem. Choose NG if the right answer is not given.

Examples

A. 0.7 x 12 =

- (A) 7.8
- (B) 8.4
- (C) 4.8
- (D) NG

B. 8.34
x 2.8

- (F) 2.335
- (G) 23.352
- (H) 1.6335
- (J) NG

 Clue In decimal problems, remember to insert the decimal point in the right place.

● Practice

1. 2.8 x 0.092 =

- (A) 2.576
- (B) 0.0257
- (C) 0.2576
- (D) NG

2. 0.3475 x 6.084 =

- (F) 21.1419
- (G) 0.4799
- (H) 2.11419
- (J) NG

3. 8
x 7.082

- (A) 5.6656
- (B) 56.656
- (C) 0.5665
- (D) NG

4. 4.877 x 1.567 =

- (F) 76.42259
- (G) 4.8765
- (H) 5.7647
- (J) NG

5. 67.04
x 0.206

- (A) 13.81024
- (B) 14.665
- (C) 16.9912
- (D) NG

6. 12 x 0.43 =

- (F) 0.516
- (G) 5.16
- (H) 6.15
- (J) NG

7. 6.35
x 0.841

- (A) 5.34035
- (B) 7.8055
- (C) 0.534035
- (D) NG

8. 9.703 x 1.08 =

- (F) 104.7924
- (G) 1.04792
- (H) 10.47924
- (J) NG

STOP

MATH: COMPUTATION

● Lesson 11: Division of Decimals

Directions: Fill in the circle for the correct answer to each problem. Choose "NG" if the right answer is not given.

Examples

A. $9\overline{)389.25}$

- (A) 4.325
- (B) 13.12
- (C) 43.25
- (D) NG

B. 59.01 ÷ 0.76

- (F) 16.8554
- (G) 77.8578
- (H) 7.76447
- (J) NG

Clue — Pay close attention when dividing decimals. It is easy to make a mistake by misplacing the decimal point.

● Practice

1. $0.44 \div 0.22 =$
- (A) 0.2
- (B) 2
- (C) 1.2
- (D) NG

2. $52 \div 3.07 =$
- (F) 17.2845
- (G) 16.93811
- (H) 1.693811
- (J) NG

3. 3.90 ÷ 3
- (A) 1.26
- (B) 13.1
- (C) 1.3
- (D) NG

4. $5\overline{)166.65}$
- (F) 33.33
- (G) 3.333
- (H) 8.923
- (J) NG

5. $3.192 \div 0.42 =$
- (A) 6.7
- (B) 0.76
- (C) 7.6
- (D) NG

6. $0.5\overline{)1.38}$
- (F) 2.96
- (G) 0.276
- (H) 27.6
- (J) NG

7. $78.6 \div 0.5 =$
- (A) 157.2
- (B) 15.27
- (C) 15.72
- (D) NG

8. $174.5 \div 3.2 =$
- (F) 34.8776
- (G) 54.53125
- (H) 5.45312
- (J) NG

STOP

Name _____   Date_____

● **Directions:** Read and work each problem. Find the correct answer. Fill in the circle for your choice.

Examples

E1. 98,788
− 23,865

(A) 67,765
(B) 74,923
(C) 77,675
(D) None of these

E2. 789 x 768 =

(F) 65,952
(G) 705,952
(H) 605,952
(J) None of these

---

1. $6.44 \div 46 =$

(A) 40.44
(B) 0.14
(C) 7.14
(D) None of these

2. $\$540.56 + \$467.48 =$

(F) $1,008.04
(G) $987.65
(H) $1,109.08
(J) None of these

3. $35 \overline{)4565}$

(A) 160R5
(B) 130R15
(C) 171
(D) None of these

4. $\dfrac{4}{9} + \dfrac{5}{6} =$

(F) $1\dfrac{1}{3}$
(G) $1\dfrac{5}{18}$
(H) $1\dfrac{4}{9}$
(J) None of these

5. $12 \div 0.75 =$

(A) 15
(B) 12.6
(C) 16
(D) None of these

6.
$1\dfrac{5}{8}$
$\text{x } 2\dfrac{3}{4}$

(F) $4\dfrac{15}{32}$
(G) $4\dfrac{3}{8}$
(H) $5\dfrac{1}{4}$
(J) None of these

7. 567 x 492 =

(A) 378,964
(B) 216,877
(C) 458,443
(D) None of these

8. $6.54 \div 3 =$

(F) 1.9
(G) 2.18
(H) 2.9
(J) None of these

9. 6,579
4,378
+ 9,512

(A) 20,475
(B) 19,675
(C) 21,435
(D) None of these

10. $\dfrac{5}{7} \div \dfrac{1}{3} =$

(F) $2\dfrac{1}{3}$
(G) $\dfrac{5}{21}$
(H) $2\dfrac{1}{7}$
(J) None of these

GO ON

MATH: COMPUTATION
SAMPLE TEST (cont.)

11.
0.3 x 61.7 =

- (A) 1.851
- (B) 18.51
- (C) 0.1851
- (D) None of these

12.
   78.45
  − 0.63

- (F) 77.82
- (G) 67.92
- (H) 78.26
- (J) None of these

13.
$9\frac{5}{6} + 4\frac{3}{8} =$

- (A) $13\frac{7}{8}$
- (B) $14\frac{5}{24}$
- (C) $11\frac{7}{24}$
- (D) None of these

14.
31.65 − 22.32 =

- (F) 7.34
- (G) 9.32
- (H) 9.33
- (J) None of these

15.
34) 569

- (A) 14R21
- (B) 16R25
- (C) 17R3
- (D) None of these

16.
56.432 ÷ 32 =

- (F) 17.635
- (G) 1.7635
- (H) 1.543
- (J) None of these

17.
   1,235
 x 4,897

- (A) 604,779
- (B) 6,047,795
- (C) 5,886,554
- (D) None of these

18.
$5\frac{1}{9} \div 2\frac{3}{4} =$

- (F) $1\frac{53}{62}$
- (G) $1\frac{55}{61}$
- (H) $1\frac{85}{99}$
- (J) None of these

19.
574.436 + 239.08 =

- (A) 8,135.16
- (B) 813.516
- (C) 814.658
- (D) None of these

20.
0.769 x 0.56 =

- (F) 0.42065
- (G) 4.3064
- (H) 0.37587
- (J) None of these

21.
   $\frac{8}{9}$
 + $\frac{1}{4}$

- (A) $1\frac{3}{32}$
- (B) $1\frac{3}{4}$
- (C) 2
- (D) None of these

22.
   321
   218
   569
 + 57

- (F) 1,163
- (G) 1,165
- (H) 1,268
- (J) None of these

STOP

Name _____   Date_____

MATH: APPLICATIONS

● Lesson 12: Geometry

Directions: Find the correct answer to each geometry problem. Fill in the circle for your answer choice.

Example

A. What is the perimeter of the figure on the right?

- (A) 34 ft.
- (B) 42 ft.
- (C) 224 ft.
- (D) 37 ft.

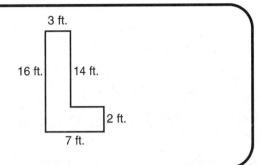

Clue Read the question carefully and think about what you are supposed to do. Then look for key words, numbers, and figures before you choose an answer.

● Practice

1. Which of the following lines are parallel?

- (A)
- (B)
- (C)
- (D)

2. Two lines in the same plane that intersect at a right angle are —

- (F) curved
- (G) perpendicular
- (H) parallel
- (J) similar

3. What is the area of a classroom that is 17 meters long and 8 meters wide?

- (A) 50 square meters
- (B) 136 square meters
- (C) 25 square meters
- (D) 9 square meters

4. The intersection of two sides of an angle is called —

- (F) the vertex
- (G) the circumference
- (H) an acute angle
- (J) a ray

GO ON

MATH: APPLICATIONS

● Lesson 12: Geometry (cont.)

5. The measure of the amount of liquid a glass can hold is called its —

- (A) volume
- (B) capacity
- (C) circumference
- (D) inside surface area

6. What is the area of the shaded shape?

□ = 1 square unit

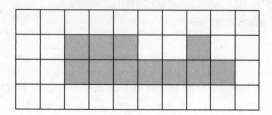

- (F) 9 square units
- (G) 8 square units
- (H) 11 square units
- (J) 22 square units

7. Which of the figures below are congruent?

A   **B**   **C**   **D**

- (A) B and C
- (B) A and C
- (C) B and D
- (D) A and D

8. Which of the angles below is acute?

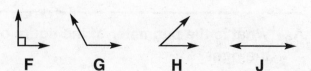

F   **G**   **H**   **J**

- (F)
- (G)
- (H)
- (J)

9. Which of these is not a cone?

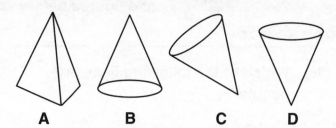

A   **B**   **C**   **D**

- (A)
- (B)
- (C)
- (D)

10. Which of these would you use to draw a circle?

- (F) compass
- (G) protractor
- (H) ruler
- (J) graph

GO ON

MATH: APPLICATIONS

Lesson 12: Geometry (cont.)

11. A right angle measures —

- (A) 180°
- (B) 90°
- (C) 360°
- (D) 60°

12. What is the volume of a rectangular prism with a length of 8 feet, a height of 6 feet, and width of 2 feet?

- (F) 16 cubic feet
- (G) 18 cubic feet
- (H) 96 cubic feet
- (J) 32 cubic feet

13. What pair of shapes below forms mirror images?

- (A) [image]
- (B) [image]
- (C) [image]
- (D) [image]

14. What pair of shapes is congruent?

- (F) [image]
- (G) [image]
- (H) [image]
- (J) [image]

15. A plane figure with 6 sides is called —

- (A) an apex
- (B) an octagon
- (C) a hexagon
- (D) a pentagon

16. What is not shown in the diagram?

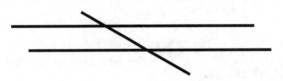

- (F) parallel lines
- (G) intersecting lines
- (H) line segment
- (J) perpendicular lines

17. Which line segment is 12 units long?

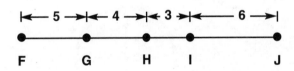

- (A) $\overline{FH}$
- (B) $\overline{GI}$
- (C) $\overline{FJ}$
- (D) $\overline{FI}$

STOP

Name _____   Date _____

MATH: APPLICATIONS

● **Lesson 13: Measurement**

Directions: Find the correct answer to each measurement problem. Fill in the circle for your choice.

Example

A. **About how many centimeters long is the pencil pictured on the right?**

    Ⓐ 5 centimeters
    Ⓑ 7 centimeters
    Ⓒ 6 centimeters
    Ⓓ 4 centimeters

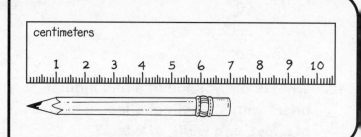

 Clue — Before you choose an answer, ask yourself if the answer makes sense. If you are confused by a problem, read it again. If you are still confused, skip the problem and come back to it later.

● **Practice**

---

1. **You go to bed at 10 P.M. You are excited because in 11 hours you are leaving for a vacation. Which clock shows what time you will be leaving for your vacation?**

2. **Betsy has 7 quarters, 8 nickels, 9 dimes, 67 pennies, and 3 half-dollars. How much money does she have altogether?**

    Ⓕ $8.43
    Ⓖ $5.22
    Ⓗ $7.32
    Ⓙ $6.22

3. **A hot dog weighs —**

    Ⓐ a few pounds
    Ⓑ a few ounces
    Ⓒ a few grams
    Ⓓ a few milligrams

4. **What fraction of a pound is 4 ounces?**

    Ⓕ $\frac{1}{8}$
    Ⓖ $\frac{1}{4}$
    Ⓗ $\frac{1}{2}$
    Ⓙ $\frac{1}{5}$

GO ON

Name _____   Date_____

● **Lesson 13: Measurement (cont.)**

5. A soccer game started at 11:15 A.M. and lasted 2 hours and 10 minutes. What time did the game end?

   (A) 1:25 A.M.
   (B) 2:25 P.M.
   (C) 1:25 P.M.
   (D) 1:35 P.M.

6. What is the ratio of four days to four weeks?

   (F) $\frac{1}{14}$
   (G) $\frac{1}{7}$
   (H) $\frac{1}{2}$
   (J) $\frac{1}{15}$

7. A map scale shows that 1 inch equals 8 miles. About how long would a section of highway be that is 4.5 inches on the map?

   (A) 36 miles
   (B) 32.5 miles
   (C) 30 miles
   (D) 18 miles

8. Which unit of measure would be best to use when weighing an adult elephant?

   (F) pounds
   (G) grams
   (H) kilograms
   (J) tons

9. Anthony's trampoline is about 3 yards across. About how many inches across is his trampoline?

   (A) 108 inches
   (B) 36 inches
   (C) 54 inches
   (D) 30 inches

10. What temperature will the thermometer show if the temperature rises 12°?

   (F) −15°
   (G) −9°
   (H) 9°
   (J) 15°

11. About how many centimeters long is this ticket stub?

   (A) 7 cm
   (B) 5 cm
   (C) 4 cm
   (D) 6 cm

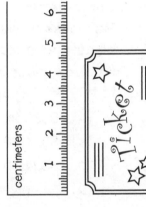

12. Stephanie is helping her mom make a bookcase. It will be 46 inches tall. Another way to describe the height of the bookcase is to say it is —

   (F) a little more than 4 feet tall
   (G) a little less than 4 feet tall
   (H) a little more than 1 meter tall
   (J) a little more than 1 yard tall

STOP

Name _____ Date_____

MATH: APPLICATIONS

● Lesson 14: Problem Solving

Directions: Find the correct answer to each problem. Mark the space for your choice.

Examples

A. Sabrina and Sophie together have more money in their piggy banks than Toby has in his. If Toby has $45 and Sabrina has $23, then Sophie must have —

- (A) less than $23.00
- (B) more than $22.00
- (C) exactly $22.00
- (D) between $21.00 and $23.00

B. Which of these numbers goes in the box to make this number sentence true?

□ < 51.06

- (F) 51.10
- (G) 51.006
- (H) 51.60
- (J) Not given

 Clue Choose "Not given" only if you are sure the right answer is not one of the choices. Look for key words, numbers, and figures in each problem, and be sure you perform the correct operation.

● Practice

1. Computer headphones cost $13.95. Ms. Jackson wants to buy 24 pairs of headphones for the school computer lab. How much will it cost altogether to buy the headphones?

- (A) $335.90
- (B) $334.80
- (C) $324.80
- (D) Not given

2. A train has 160 seats. Passengers are in 97 of them. Which equation would you use to find out how many seats are empty?

- (F) 160 ÷ 97 = □
- (G) 160 − 97 = □
- (H) 160 + 97 = □
- (J) 160 x 97 = □

3. There are 2,464 monkeys in a nature preserve. They live in groups of 16. How many groups of monkeys are there?

- (A) 154 groups
- (B) 164 groups
- (C) 153 groups
- (D) Not given

4. Mason, Clare, and Clark each bought candy in the bulk food store. The candy they bought weighed $2\frac{3}{4}$ pounds, $4\frac{5}{6}$ pounds, and $3\frac{7}{8}$ pounds. How many pounds of candy did they buy in all?

- (F) $12\frac{11}{12}$
- (G) $11\frac{1}{24}$
- (H) $10\frac{11}{24}$
- (J) Not given

GO ON

Name _____   Date_____

MATH: APPLICATIONS

● Lesson 14: Problem Solving (cont.)

Mr. VanderSy's class earned $582.00 during the school year in order to purchase new books for the library. The graph below shows the percentage of money earned from each activity. Use it to answer questions 5, 6, and 7.

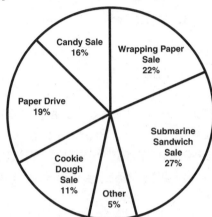

5. Which fundraiser earned the most money?

    Ⓐ   the candy sale

    Ⓑ   the wrapping paper sale

    Ⓒ   the submarine sandwich sale

    Ⓓ   the paper drive

6. How much money was earned from the cookie dough sale?

    Ⓕ $63.02

    Ⓖ $123.02

    Ⓗ $64.02

    Ⓙ $73.03

7. How much less was earned on the paper drive than from the wrapping paper sale?

    Ⓐ $17.46

    Ⓑ $23.46

    Ⓒ $18.46

    Ⓓ $16.46

8. Angelica is helping her dad build a deck. The surface of the deck will be 12 feet wide and 14 feet long. The boards they are using can cover an area of 4 square feet each. Which of these shows how many boards they will need to cover the surface of the deck?

    Ⓕ $(12 \times 14) \div 4 = \square$

    Ⓖ $(12 \times 14) \times 4 = \square$

    Ⓗ $12 + 14 + 4 = \square$

    Ⓙ $(12 \div 14) \times 4 = \square$

9. Darnell's speech took $12\frac{3}{4}$ minutes. Tara's speech lasted $\frac{8}{12}$ as long. How long was Tara's speech?

    Ⓐ   9 minutes

    Ⓑ $8\frac{1}{2}$ minutes

    Ⓒ   11 minutes

    Ⓓ $9\frac{1}{2}$ minutes

10. Aleesha saved $0.45 out of her allowance for several weeks so that she could buy a bottle of nail polish for $2.70. How many weeks did she need to save $0.45?

    Ⓕ   6 weeks

    Ⓖ   4 weeks

    Ⓗ   3 weeks

    Ⓙ   5 weeks

11. Tony, a novice jogger, in his first week ran $\frac{1}{2}$ mile on his first try, $1\frac{1}{4}$ mile on his second try, and 2 miles on his third try. How far would Tony run in total in two weeks if he ran the same distances the next week?

    Ⓐ $3\frac{3}{4}$ miles

    Ⓑ $7\frac{1}{2}$ miles

    Ⓒ $6\frac{3}{4}$ miles

    Ⓓ $8\frac{1}{2}$ miles

GO ON

1-57768-976-3 *Spectrum Test Practice 6*

MATH: APPLICATIONS

● Lesson 14: Problem Solving (cont.)

The soccer team members needed to buy their own shin guards, socks, shoes, and shorts. Two players volunteered to do some comparative shopping to find the store with the best deals. Use their charts to answer questions 12–14.

Sports Corner

Socks	.3 pairs for $9.30
Shoes	.2 pairs for $48.24
Shin Guards	.4 pairs for $32.48
Shorts	.5 pairs for $60.30

Sam's Soccer Supplies

Socks	2 pairs for $6.84
Shoes	3 pairs for $84.15
Shin Guards	5 pairs for $35.70
Shorts	4 pairs for $36.36

12. **How much does it cost for one pair of shin guards at the store with the best deal?**

   (F) $7.14
   (G) $8.12
   (H) $32.48
   (J) $4.76

13. **How much would it cost to buy one pair of shoes and socks at Sports Corner?**

   (A) $27.22
   (B) $57.54
   (C) $31.47
   (D) $28.22

14. **How much would it cost to buy one pair of shoes and socks at Sam's Soccer Supplies?**

   (F) $27.22
   (G) $31.47
   (H) $29.11
   (J) $31.57

15. **It takes 5 workers about 50 hours to build a house. How long would it take if there were 10 workers?**

   (A) 25 hours
   (B) $12\frac{1}{2}$ hours
   (C) 100 hours
   (D) Not given

16. **There are 10 white socks and 10 black socks in a drawer. Bruce reaches into his drawer without looking. What is the probability that he will pick a white sock?**

   (F) $\frac{1}{2}$
   (G) $\frac{1}{3}$
   (H) $\frac{1}{4}$
   (J) Not given

17. **A group of teachers are ordering sandwiches from the deli. They can choose ham, beef, turkey, or bologna on white bread, wheat bread, or rye bread. How many different meat and bread combinations are possible?**

   (A) 12
   (B) 16
   (C) 7
   (D) Not given

GO ON

MATH: APPLICATIONS

● Lesson 14: Problem Solving (cont.)

The graph below shows the average number of rainy days per month in Sun City, Florida. Use the graph to answer questions 18–20.

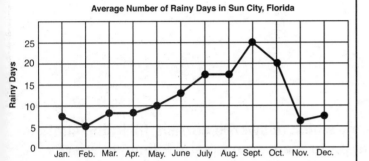

Average Number of Rainy Days in Sun City, Florida

18. Based on this graph, which two months should have been the best for tourists?

    (F) January and February

    (G) February and November

    (H) March and April

    (J) April and December

19. Which two-month period shows the greatest change in the number of rainy days?

    (A) May and June

    (B) June and July

    (C) October and November

    (D) August and September

20. How many inches of rain fell during the rainiest month?

    (F) 20 inches

    (G) 25 inches

    (H) about 18 inches

    (J) Not given

21. 14 teachers and 246 students will travel to the state capitol. One bus holds 38 people. How many buses are needed altogether?

    (A) 6 buses

    (B) 7 buses

    (C) 5 buses

    (D) 8 buses

22. Last summer, 6 friends ran their own lawn care business. The friends made a total of $498.54. The friends agreed to share the profit equally. How much did each friend make?

    (F) $73.09

    (G) $83.09

    (H) $84.09

    (J) $79.09

23. Mike received 65% of the votes cast for class treasurer. What fractional part of the votes did Mike receive?

    (A) $\frac{13}{20}$

    (B) $\frac{12}{19}$

    (C) $\frac{11}{20}$

    (D) Not given

24. Marty made a base hit on 25% of his official times at bat. What is his batting average? (Note: Batting averages are usually expressed as thousandths.)

    (F) .450

    (G) .250

    (H) .025

    (J) .275

STOP

Name _____ Date_____

MATH: APPLICATIONS

● **Lesson 15: Algebra**

Directions: Find the correct answer to each measurement problem. Fill in the circle for your choice.

Examples

A. What is the value of *z* in the number sentence 12 x *z* =144?

- Ⓐ 8
- Ⓑ 12
- Ⓒ 122
- Ⓓ 11

B. If 6 < *f* and *f* < *g*, what should replace the box in 6 ☐ *g*?

- Ⓕ <
- Ⓖ >
- Ⓗ −
- Ⓙ =

If you are sure you know which answer is correct, fill in the circle for your answer and move on to the next problem. Eliminate answer choices you know are wrong.

● **Practice**

1. Which statement is true if *b* is a whole number?
   - Ⓐ If *b* − 8 = 16, then 8 + *b* = 16
   - Ⓑ If 8 x *b* = 16, then 16 ÷ *b* = 8
   - Ⓒ If 8 ÷ *b* = 16, then 16 x 8 = *b*
   - Ⓓ If 8 + *b* = 16, then 16 + 8 = *b*

2. If *y* > 98 and *y* < 123, which of the following is a possible value of *y*?
   - Ⓕ 124
   - Ⓖ 108
   - Ⓗ 97
   - Ⓙ 221

3. What is the value of *x* if 54 ÷ *x* = 9?
   - Ⓐ 7
   - Ⓑ 6
   - Ⓒ 63
   - Ⓓ 45

4. What point is at (6,2)?
   - Ⓕ M
   - Ⓖ N
   - Ⓗ O
   - Ⓙ P

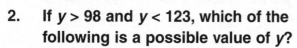

5. 13 people ride to school in 2 cars. One car holds three more people than the other. How many people are in each car?
   - Ⓐ 8 in one car and 5 in the other
   - Ⓑ 9 in one car and 4 in the other
   - Ⓒ 7 in one car and 6 in the other
   - Ⓓ 3 in one car and 10 in the other

STOP

Name _____   Date _____

MATH: APPLICATIONS
SAMPLE TEST

● **Directions:** Read and work each problem. Find and fill in the correct answer choice.

Examples

E1. The enrollment at King School has increased 20% from last year. The enrollment last year was 650. By how many students has the enrollment increased?

- Ⓐ 120
- Ⓑ 130
- Ⓒ 150
- Ⓓ 90

E2. How many quarts are in 6 gallons?

- Ⓕ 48
- Ⓖ 24
- Ⓗ 16
- Ⓙ 12

---

1. What is the perimeter of this rectangle?

- Ⓐ 42 cm
- Ⓑ 84 cm
- Ⓒ 432 cm
- Ⓓ 82 cm

18 cm ▭ 24 cm

2. A VCR normally costs $119. It is on sale for $99. How much would you save if you bought 2 VCRs on sale?

- Ⓕ ($119 + $99) x 2 = ☐
- Ⓖ ($119 − $99) ÷ 2 = ☐
- Ⓗ ($119 − $99) x 2 = ☐
- Ⓙ ($119 + $99) ÷ 2 = ☐

3. Sven went grocery shopping with his mother. The groceries totaled $36.37. Sven's mom paid for the food with two $20 bills. Which of these is the correct amount of change she should receive?

- Ⓐ 2 one-dollar bills, two quarters, two dimes, and three pennies
- Ⓑ 3 one-dollar bills, two quarters, one dime, and three pennies
- Ⓒ 3 one-dollar bills, three quarters, one nickel, and three pennies
- Ⓓ Not given

4. One box of nails weighs 3.6 pounds and another box weighs 5.4 pounds. How much more does the heavier box weigh?

- Ⓕ 1.8 pounds
- Ⓖ 1.6 pounds
- Ⓗ 18 pounds
- Ⓙ 1.2 pounds

5. Your uncle bought 375 feet of wire fencing. He put up 325 feet today and saved the rest for tomorrow. Which equation shows how many feet of fencing he has left?

- Ⓐ 375 + ☐ = 325
- Ⓑ 375 − 325 = ☐
- Ⓒ ☐ = 375 + 325
- Ⓓ 375 − ☐ = 325

6. What is the value of r if 17 x r = 68?

- Ⓕ 51
- Ⓖ 4
- Ⓗ 85
- Ⓙ 6

GO ON ⟩

Name _____   Date _____

The chart below shows how the space in a store was divided among the different departments. Use the chart to answer numbers 7–9.

frozen foods 1/4
fresh produce 1/8
meat & deli 1/10
packaged foods 1/5
bakery ?
beverages 1/5

7. What fraction of the space in the store is the bakery?

    (A) $\frac{1}{4}$

    (B) $\frac{1}{8}$

    (C) $\frac{1}{5}$

    (D) $\frac{1}{10}$

8. What percentage of the space in the store is devoted to frozen foods?

    (F) 30%

    (G) 25%

    (H) 40%

    (J) 12.5%

9. If the total space in the store is 3,000 square feet, how many square feet of space is taken up by packaged foods?

    (A) 400 square feet

    (B) 550 square feet

    (C) 600 square feet

    (D) 60 square feet

10. Which of these shows a radius?

    (F)

    (G)

    (H)
       D   E

    (J)

11. Phil's van is 1.7 meters tall. About how many millimeters tall is it?

    (A) 170

    (B) 1,700

    (C) 17,000

    (D) Not given

12. A shoe box is 6 inches wide, 11 inches long, and 5 inches high. What is the volume of the box?

    (F) 330 cubic inches

    (G) 22 cubic inches

    (H) 230 cubic inches

    (J) Not given

GO ON

Name _____   Date_____

The graph below shows the average basketball attendance for the season. Use the graph to answer numbers 13–15.

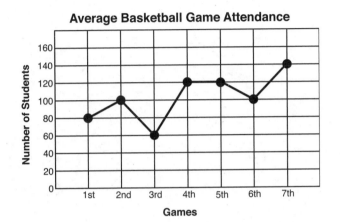

Average Basketball Game Attendance

13. **What was the increase in attendance from the first to the seventh game?**
    - (A) 50 students
    - (B) 60 students
    - (C) 140 students
    - (D) 70 students

14. **Between which two games was there the smallest increase in attendance?**
    - (F) 1st and 2nd games
    - (G) 6th and 7th games
    - (H) 5th and 6th games
    - (J) 2nd and 3rd games

15. **How many students altogether attended games?**
    - (A) 140 students
    - (B) 160 students
    - (C) 720 students
    - (D) 600 students

16. **Joanne kept track of the rainfall for one week. She recorded 0.8 inch on Monday, 0.5 inch on Tuesday, and 0.5 inch on Friday. How much rain fell during the week?**
    - (F) 1.5 inches
    - (G) 2 inches
    - (H) 3 inches
    - (J) 1.8 inches

17. **Chris put 72 kilograms of jam into jars. He put 0.4 kilogram into each jar. How many jars did he use?**
    - (A) 90 jars
    - (B) 180 jars
    - (C) 80 jars
    - (D) Not given

18. **What is the area of the shape below?**

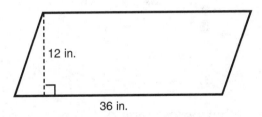

12 in.

36 in.

    - (F) 532 in.²
    - (G) 432 in.²
    - (H) 48 in.²
    - (J) 96 in.²

GO ON

Name _____ Date_____

19. About how long is the paper clip above the ruler?

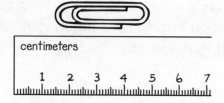

- (A) 3.5 cm
- (B) 4 cm
- (C) 4.5 cm
- (D) Not given

20. What is the perimeter of the shaded figure below?

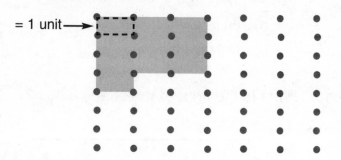

- (F) 9 units
- (G) 14 units
- (H) 11 units
- (J) 15 units

21. The area of Mr. White's classroom is 981.75 square feet. The gym is 4.50 times as large. What is the area of the gym?

- (A) 4,500.12 square feet
- (B) 4,417.875 square feet
- (C) 986.25 square feet
- (D) 4,411.78 square feet

22. Which clock shows the time 3 hours and 15 minutes before midnight?

 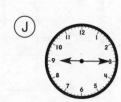

23. Jeremy opened a savings account. He deposited $23.45 into his account. The monthly rate of interest on his account is 5%. How much interest would Jeremy receive on that amount at the end of the month?

- (A) $1.17
- (B) $117.25
- (C) $17.25
- (D) $0.17

24. Micah is shipping a gift to his grandpa. The box he needs to ship the gift must have a volume of at least 130 cubic inches but not more than 160 cubic inches. Which of these boxes could he use?

- (F) a 5 in. x 3 in. x 5 in. box
- (G) a 4 in. x 6 in. x 5 in. box
- (H) a 6 in. x 4 in. x 6 in. box
- (J) a 5 in. x 5 in. x 5 in. box

STOP

ANSWER SHEET

STUDENT'S NAME			SCHOOL
LAST	FIRST	MI	TEACHER

FEMALE ◯   MALE ◯

BIRTH DATE

MONTH	DAY	YEAR

JAN ◯
FEB ◯
MAR ◯
APR ◯
MAY ◯
JUN ◯
JUL ◯
AUG ◯
SEP ◯
OCT ◯
NOV ◯
DEC ◯

GRADE
⑤ ⑥ ⑦

Part 1: CONCEPTS

E1 Ⓐ Ⓑ Ⓒ Ⓓ		6 Ⓕ Ⓖ Ⓗ Ⓙ		13 Ⓐ Ⓑ Ⓒ Ⓓ		20 Ⓕ Ⓖ Ⓗ Ⓙ	
E2 Ⓕ Ⓖ Ⓗ Ⓙ		7 Ⓐ Ⓑ Ⓒ Ⓓ		14 Ⓕ Ⓖ Ⓗ Ⓙ		21 Ⓐ Ⓑ Ⓒ Ⓓ	
1 Ⓐ Ⓑ Ⓒ Ⓓ		8 Ⓕ Ⓖ Ⓗ Ⓙ		15 Ⓐ Ⓑ Ⓒ Ⓓ		22 Ⓕ Ⓖ Ⓗ Ⓙ	
2 Ⓕ Ⓖ Ⓗ Ⓙ		9 Ⓐ Ⓑ Ⓒ Ⓓ		16 Ⓕ Ⓖ Ⓗ Ⓙ		23 Ⓐ Ⓑ Ⓒ Ⓓ	
3 Ⓐ Ⓑ Ⓒ Ⓓ		10 Ⓕ Ⓖ Ⓗ Ⓙ		17 Ⓐ Ⓑ Ⓒ Ⓓ		24 Ⓕ Ⓖ Ⓗ Ⓙ	
4 Ⓕ Ⓖ Ⓗ Ⓙ		11 Ⓐ Ⓑ Ⓒ Ⓓ		18 Ⓕ Ⓖ Ⓗ Ⓙ		25 Ⓐ Ⓑ Ⓒ Ⓓ	
5 Ⓐ Ⓑ Ⓒ Ⓓ		12 Ⓕ Ⓖ Ⓗ Ⓙ		19 Ⓐ Ⓑ Ⓒ Ⓓ			

Part 2: COMPUTATION

E1 Ⓐ Ⓑ Ⓒ Ⓓ		6 Ⓕ Ⓖ Ⓗ Ⓙ		13 Ⓐ Ⓑ Ⓒ Ⓓ		20 Ⓕ Ⓖ Ⓗ Ⓙ	
E2 Ⓕ Ⓖ Ⓗ Ⓙ		7 Ⓐ Ⓑ Ⓒ Ⓓ		14 Ⓕ Ⓖ Ⓗ Ⓙ		21 Ⓐ Ⓑ Ⓒ Ⓓ	
1 Ⓐ Ⓑ Ⓒ Ⓓ		8 Ⓕ Ⓖ Ⓗ Ⓙ		15 Ⓐ Ⓑ Ⓒ Ⓓ		22 Ⓕ Ⓖ Ⓗ Ⓙ	
2 Ⓕ Ⓖ Ⓗ Ⓙ		9 Ⓐ Ⓑ Ⓒ Ⓓ		16 Ⓕ Ⓖ Ⓗ Ⓙ			
3 Ⓐ Ⓑ Ⓒ Ⓓ		10 Ⓕ Ⓖ Ⓗ Ⓙ		17 Ⓐ Ⓑ Ⓒ Ⓓ			
4 Ⓕ Ⓖ Ⓗ Ⓙ		11 Ⓐ Ⓑ Ⓒ Ⓓ		18 Ⓕ Ⓖ Ⓗ Ⓙ			
5 Ⓐ Ⓑ Ⓒ Ⓓ		12 Ⓕ Ⓖ Ⓗ Ⓙ		19 Ⓐ Ⓑ Ⓒ Ⓓ			

Part 3: APPLICATIONS

E1 Ⓐ Ⓑ Ⓒ Ⓓ		6 Ⓕ Ⓖ Ⓗ Ⓙ		13 Ⓐ Ⓑ Ⓒ Ⓓ	
E2 Ⓕ Ⓖ Ⓗ Ⓙ		7 Ⓐ Ⓑ Ⓒ Ⓓ		14 Ⓕ Ⓖ Ⓗ Ⓙ	
1 Ⓐ Ⓑ Ⓒ Ⓓ		8 Ⓕ Ⓖ Ⓗ Ⓙ		15 Ⓐ Ⓑ Ⓒ Ⓓ	
2 Ⓕ Ⓖ Ⓗ Ⓙ		9 Ⓐ Ⓑ Ⓒ Ⓓ		16 Ⓕ Ⓖ Ⓗ Ⓙ	
3 Ⓐ Ⓑ Ⓒ Ⓓ		10 Ⓕ Ⓖ Ⓗ Ⓙ		17 Ⓐ Ⓑ Ⓒ Ⓓ	
4 Ⓕ Ⓖ Ⓗ Ⓙ		11 Ⓐ Ⓑ Ⓒ Ⓓ		18 Ⓕ Ⓖ Ⓗ Ⓙ	
5 Ⓐ Ⓑ Ⓒ Ⓓ		12 Ⓕ Ⓖ Ⓗ Ⓙ			

1-57768-976-3 *Spectrum Test Practice 6*

MATH PRACTICE TEST

● Part 1: Concepts

Directions: Read and work each problem. Find the correct answer. Fill in the circle for your choice.

Examples

E1. $\frac{9}{1,000} =$

- (A) 9.000
- (B) 0.9000
- (C) 0.0900
- (D) 0.0090

E2. Which two numbers are both factors of 48?

- (F) 4, 9
- (G) 4, 7
- (H) 8, 12
- (J) 6, 18

---

1. Which figure has the same shaded area as figure A?

fig. A

(A)

(B)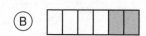

(C)

(D)

2. Which number is ten thousand more than 399,587?

- (F) 400,587
- (G) 409,587
- (H) 499,587
- (D) 490,587

3. What is another name for 60?

- (A) (4 x 6) x 6
- (B) 6 x (4 + 6)
- (C) (20 x 2) ÷ 2
- (D) 4 x (18 ÷ 3)

4. Which fraction is another name for $\frac{2}{5}$?

- (F) $\frac{16}{40}$
- (G) $\frac{4}{40}$
- (H) $\frac{4}{15}$
- (J) $\frac{12}{48}$

5. Point J is closest in value to —

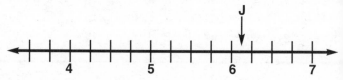

- (A) 6.2
- (B) 6.5
- (C) 6.125
- (D) 7.5

6. What number is missing from the pattern shown below?

8, 10, 14, 20, __, 38, 50

- (F) 24
- (G) 26
- (H) 28
- (J) 25

1-57768-976-3 *Spectrum Test Practice 6*

MATH PRACTICE TEST
Part 1: Concepts (cont.)

7. Which of these does not have the same value as the others?

   (A) $\frac{24}{3}$

   (B) $\sqrt{64}$

   (C) 32 x 0.25

   (D) 0.08

8. How many of the fractions in the box are greater than $\frac{3}{5}$?

$\frac{2}{5}$	$\frac{3}{4}$	$\frac{6}{7}$	$\frac{1}{2}$	$\frac{20}{25}$	$\frac{7}{10}$

   (F) 1

   (G) 3

   (H) 4

   (J) 2

9. Which of these statements is true about the number 378,654?

   (A) It has a 3 in the thousands place and a 4 in the ones place.

   (B) It has a 7 in the ten thousands place and a 6 in the tens place.

   (C) It has a 3 in the hundred thousands place and a 5 in the tens place.

   (D) It has an 8 in the ten thousands place and a 6 in the hundreds place.

10. What should replace the box in the number sentence below?

    (7 x □) − 9 = 54

    (F) 8

    (G) 7

    (H) 5

    (J) 9

11. What statement is true about the number sentence 798 ÷ 10 = □?

    (A) □ is more than 80.

    (B) □ is more than 90.

    (C) □ is less than 80.

    (D) □ is more than 700.

12. Which fraction is in its simplest form?

    (F) $\frac{9}{12}$

    (G) $\frac{12}{20}$

    (H) $\frac{4}{5}$

    (J) $\frac{2}{8}$

13. Which is a multiple of 15?

    (A) 55

    (B) 45

    (C) 70

    (D) 5

14. Which of these is an improper fraction?

    (F) $\frac{45}{90}$

    (G) $\frac{37}{36}$

    (H) $1\frac{2}{9}$

    (J) $\frac{9}{10}$

15. $\sqrt{81}$

    (A) 11

    (B) 7

    (C) 8

    (D) 9

GO ON

16. Which of these is another name for $\frac{13}{4}$?

   (F) 4

   (G) $3\frac{1}{3}$

   (H) $8\frac{1}{4}$

   (J) $3\frac{1}{4}$

17. Estimate the sum of 369 plus 547. Round both numbers to the nearest ten and solve. Then round to the nearest hundred and solve. What are the estimated sums?

   (A) 920 and 900

   (B) 890 and 900

   (C) 910 and 900

   (D) 900 and 1000

18. Mary has 6 apples, Sara has 5 oranges, and Kate has 4 bananas. What fraction of the fruit does Sara have?

   (F) $\frac{1}{15}$

   (G) $\frac{1}{3}$

   (H) $\frac{1}{5}$

   (J) $\frac{3}{5}$

19. Which of these is a prime number?

   (A) 33

   (B) 11

   (C) 18

   (D) 32

20. Which of these is 0.494 rounded to the nearest tenth?

   (F) 0.4

   (G) 0.5

   (H) 0.410

   (J) 0.510

21. Which is the least whole number that makes the number sentence below true?

$$6 \times \square < 70$$

   (A) 12

   (B) 10

   (C) 13

   (D) 11

22. What should replace the $\square$ in the number sentence below?

$$8 \times 7 = (6 \times 6) + (4 \times \square)$$

   (F) 4

   (G) 6

   (H) 5

   (J) 7

23. Which of these is the expanded numeral for 57,076?

   (A) 50,000 + 7,000 + 70 + 6

   (B) 5,000 + 70 + 6

   (C) 5,700 + 70 + 6

   (D) 50,000 + 700 + 6

24. What does the underlined numeral name?

456,7<u>8</u>6,774

   (F) millions

   (G) hundred millions

   (H) ten thousands

   (J) ten millions

25. Which of these numbers shows $\frac{29}{7}$ as a mixed fraction?

   (A) $4\frac{1}{7}$

   (B) $\frac{7}{29}$

   (C) $4\frac{2}{7}$

   (D) 0.34

STOP

MATH PRACTICE TEST

● **Part 2: Computation**

Directions: Find the correct answer to each problem. Mark the space for your choice.

Examples

E1. $40\overline{)1200}$

(A) 300
(B) 30
(C) 3
(D) None of these

E2. $8.3 + 0.7 = \square$

(F) 8.37
(G) 9
(H) 8.73
(J) None of these

1. $6,788 + 3,528 + 6,743 =$

(A) 17,059
(B) 16,059
(C) 17,058
(D) None of these

2. 7,500
   x 60

(F) 45,000
(G) 450,000
(H) 420,500
(J) None of these

3. $896 \div 33 =$

(A) 28R2
(B) 27R5
(C) 27
(D) None of these

4. $\frac{5}{9} \times \frac{3}{8} =$

(F) $\frac{4}{9}$
(G) $\frac{5}{12}$
(H) $\frac{5}{24}$
(J) None of these

5. 92,654
   − 43,879

(A) 4,877
(B) 67,775
(C) 48,775
(D) None of these

6. $6\overline{)4,387}$

(F) 731R1
(G) 731
(H) 732R2
(J) None of these

7. $994 \times 738 =$

(A) 732,572
(B) 723,572
(C) 833,572
(D) None of these

8. 77.59
   − 5.8

(F) 72.79
(G) 71.79
(H) 72.68
(J) None of these

9. $\frac{8}{9} - \frac{3}{6} =$

(A) $\frac{7}{8}$
(B) $\frac{5}{6}$
(C) $\frac{7}{18}$
(D) None of these

10. $3.4 + 7.5 + 0.9 =$

(F) 12.6
(G) 11.8
(H) 14.2
(J) None of these

GO ON

MATH PRACTICE TEST
Part 2: Computation (cont.)

11.
$$5\frac{3}{4}$$
$$+\,1\frac{4}{7}$$

(A) $6\frac{8}{9}$

(B) $7\frac{1}{4}$

(C) $7\frac{9}{28}$

(D) None of these

12. $(3 + 7) - (3 \times 7) \div 7 =$

(F) 8

(G) 7R8

(H) 7

(J) None of these

13. $25.5 \div 3 =$

(A) 7.6

(B) 8.5

(C) 7.5

(D) None of these

14.
$$8,976$$
$$\times\ 60$$

(F) 53,856

(G) 438,560

(H) 538,560

(J) None of these

15. $13\overline{)549.9}$

(A) 41.3

(B) 42.6

(C) 51.41

(D) None of these

16.
$$8\frac{1}{12}$$
$$-\,6\frac{3}{4}$$

(F) $1\frac{1}{3}$

(G) $2\frac{3}{4}$

(H) $1\frac{1}{12}$

(J) None of these

17. $45.6 + 33.9 =$

(A) 78.5

(B) 79.4

(C) 79.5

(D) None of these

18. $245 \times 8 =$

(F) 2,453

(G) 1,985

(H) 1,960

(J) None of these

19.
$$\frac{7}{9}$$
$$+\ \frac{11}{18}$$

(A) $1\frac{7}{18}$

(B) $\frac{17}{18}$

(C) $1\frac{7}{9}$

(D) None of these

20.
$$45,603$$
$$-\,44,984$$

(F) 719

(G) 818

(H) 619

(J) None of these

21. $(8 \times 9 - 5 \times 9) \div 4 =$

(A) 6

(B) 6R3

(C) 5R9

(D) None of these

22.
$$5\frac{3}{4}$$
$$+\,7\frac{2}{3}$$

(F) $13\frac{5}{12}$

(G) $12\frac{3}{4}$

(H) $13\frac{1}{3}$

(J) None of these

STOP

MATH PRACTICE TEST

● **Part 3: Applications**

Directions: Read and work each problem. Find the correct answer. Fill in the circle for your choice.

Examples

E1. How much change will you receive from $5.00 if you buy a shake for $1.29, a hamburger for $0.99, and fries for $0.89?

- (A) $1.82
- (B) $1.83
- (C) $3.71
- (D) $2.83

E2. If 27 students each brought in 6 cookies, which equation shows how many cookies they brought in all?

- (F) 27 + 6 = □
- (G) 27 x 6 = □
- (H) 27 − 6 = □
- (J) 27 ÷ 6 = □

1. Diane lives in an apartment that is 6 stories tall. About how tall is the building?
   - (A) 60 feet
   - (B) 100 feet
   - (C) 600 feet
   - (D) 10 feet

2. Which equation shows the total attendance at the Science Fair if 67 girls and 59 boys attended?
   - (F) 67 − 59 = □
   - (G) 67 + 59 = □
   - (H) 67 ÷ 59 = □
   - (J) 67 x 59 = □

3. Which of these statements is true?
   - (A) 11 quarters is worth more than 19 dimes
   - (B) 50 nickels is worth more than 25 dimes
   - (C) 6 quarters is worth more than 16 dimes
   - (D) 15 nickels is worth more than 9 dimes

4. If $z + 8 = 31$, then $z = $ □
   - (F) 39
   - (G) 23
   - (H) 22
   - (J) 4

5. What is the perimeter of this rectangle?
   - (A) 62 cm
   - (B) 31 cm
   - (C) 168 cm
   - (D) Not given

   24 cm
   7 cm

6. A carpenter has 12 pieces of wood that are each 9 feet long. He has to cut 2 feet from each piece of wood because of water damage. Which equation shows how much good wood is left?
   - (F) (9 + 2) x 12 = □
   - (G) (12 − 2) x 9 = □
   - (H) (12 x 9) − 2 = □
   - (J) (9 − 2) x 12 = □

7. Pizzazz Pizza Parlor gave the sixth-grade class a 25% discount on pizzas they purchased for a party. Each pizza originally cost $12.00. How much did the sixth graders pay per pizza?
   - (A) $3.00
   - (B) $9.00
   - (C) $8.00
   - (D) $6.00

GO ON

Name _____ Date _____

MATH PRACTICE TEST
Part 3: Applications (cont.)

The graph below shows the number of dogs registered with the American Canine Club in 1998 and 1999. Use the graph to do numbers 8–9.

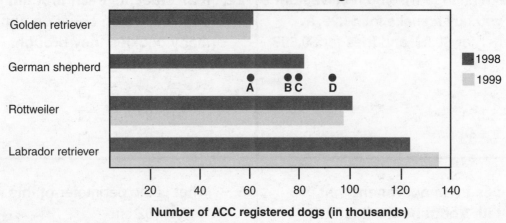

American Canine Club Registration

8. The number of registered Labrador retrievers in 1998 was —
   - (F) between 100,000 and 120,000
   - (G) less than 100,000
   - (H) between 120,000 and 140,000
   - (J) more than 140,000

9. The number of registered German shepherds in 1999 was 62,006. Look at points A, B, C, and D on the graph. Which point indicates where a bar should be drawn to complete the graph?
   - (A) point A
   - (B) point B
   - (C) point C
   - (D) point D

10. Suppose you wrote the word **VACATION** on a strip of paper and cut the paper into pieces with one letter per piece. If you put the pieces into a hat and pulled out one piece without looking, what is the probability that you would pick out the letter A?

   - (F) 1 out of 8
   - (G) 2 out of 8
   - (H) 4 out of 5
   - (J) 2 out of 7

11. **Which pair of shapes is congruent?**

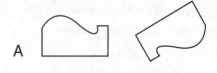

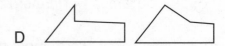

12. **130 inches is —**
   - (F) exactly 10 feet
   - (G) more than 3 yards
   - (H) between 9 and 10 feet
   - (J) less than 3 yards

Name _____ Date_____

MATH PRACTICE TEST
Part 3: Applications (cont.)

13. What fraction of 1 week is 12 hours?

(A) $\frac{1}{12}$

(B) $\frac{1}{14}$

(C) $\frac{1}{24}$

(D) $\frac{1}{8}$

14. What is the perimeter of the rectangle below?

(F) 38 in.

(G) 76 in.

(H) 336 in.

(J) 10 in.

24 in.

14 in.

15. Jupiter has 16 moons, Mars has $\frac{1}{8}$ the number of moons that Jupiter has. How many moons does Mars have?

(A) 8

(B) 2

(C) 4

(D) 6

16. Connie earned $6.00 by baby-sitting. She added that money to some allowance she had saved and bought a new video game for $22.79. She had $2.88 left over. How much allowance had Connie saved?

(F) $19.91

(G) $13.78

(H) $19.67

(J) $18.77

17. School begins at 8:45 A.M. The sixth graders eat lunch 2 hours and 45 minutes later. Lunch lasts 30 minutes. Which clock shows the time the sixth graders return to class after eating lunch?

(A)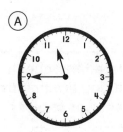

(B)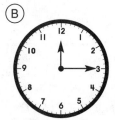

(C)

(D)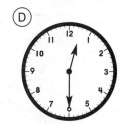

18. A room is 18^2 feet. What is the area of the room?

(F) 36 square feet

(G) 324 square feet

(H) 72 square feet

(J) 648 square feet

STOP

Published by Spectrum. Copyright protected.
1-57768-976-3 *Spectrum Test Practice 6*

SCIENCE

● Lesson 1: Concepts

Directions: Read each question. Fill in the circle for the correct answer.

Examples

A. Which of these is not a mammal?

- (A) elephant
- (B) whale
- (C) iguana
- (D) mouse

B. Which animal would not be found in a pond ecosystem?

- (F) heron
- (G) fish
- (H) dragonfly
- (J) monkey

 Clue Read the questions carefully before choosing an answer. If you are unsure of your answer, begin by eliminating answer choices you know are wrong.

● Practice

1. What kind of charge do protons carry?

- (A) negative
- (B) positive
- (C) neutral
- (D) electric

2. Which is the gland that produces hormones?

- (F) pituitary
- (G) heart
- (H) large intestine
- (J) kidney

3. Which animal would be lowest on a food chain?

- (A) frog
- (B) mosquito
- (C) duck
- (D) man

4. Which gas do mammals exhale?

- (F) oxygen
- (G) hydrogen
- (H) carbon dioxide
- (J) methane

5. What is the name of the moon's changing shapes?

- (A) orbits
- (B) phases
- (C) eclipses
- (D) stages

6. What is the name of the process by which plants take in carbon dioxide and water to make food?

- (F) cell division
- (G) biology
- (H) photosynthesis
- (J) respiration

7. Which of these is an example of camouflage?

- (A) The stick insect resembles the twig on which it sits.
- (B) The young joey grows and develops in its mother's pouch.
- (C) The anteater has a long, slender snout and a long tongue, which it can thrust into anthills.
- (D) The porcupine is covered with long sharp quills.

GO ON

SCIENCE

● **Lesson 1: Concepts (cont.)**

8. **Which is the organ that pumps blood through the body?**
   - (F) lung
   - (G) heart
   - (H) liver
   - (J) brain

9. **Which of these is not a vertebrate?**
   - (A) fish
   - (B) snake
   - (C) worm
   - (D) toad

10. **Which of these trees is not a conifer?**
    - (F) pine
    - (G) fir
    - (H) cedar
    - (J) oak

11. **Which of these is not a type of rock?**
    - (A) metamorphic
    - (B) fragmentary
    - (C) sedimentary
    - (D) igneous

12. **What is the name of the energy from the sun?**
    - (F) solar
    - (G) polar
    - (H) ocular
    - (J) lunar

13. **What is the name of the female part of a plant?**
    - (A) stamen
    - (B) pistil
    - (C) petal
    - (D) sepal

14. **Which of these is not part of the eye?**
    - (F) pupil
    - (G) cornea
    - (H) lens
    - (J) anvil

15. **Which of these is the innermost layer of the earth?**
    - (A) mantle
    - (B) core
    - (C) crust
    - (D) trench

STOP

SCIENCE

● Lesson 2: Applications

Directions: Read the passage below carefully. Then use it to answer the questions. Write a short answer for each question.

Examples

Some behavior is learned, and some behavior is innate or inborn. Innate behavior is behavior you know without having to be taught. A baby cannot read or write, but a baby knows how to cry from the moment it is born. Crying is an inborn behavior. Like people, animals have both learned and inborn behaviors.

E1. A. **Name one inborn behavior.**

_____

B. **Name one learned behavior.**

_____

 Clue Skim the passage so you have an understanding of what it is about. Then skim the questions. Answer the easiest questions first.

● Practice

The human ear has three parts: the outer ear (which is the part you see), the middle ear, and the inner ear. The outer ear collects sound waves and funnels them to the middle ear in a way very similar to a satellite dish antenna. The outer ear is attached to an opening called the auditory canal. The sound waves are channeled to the eardrum. The eardrum vibrates against the three small bones of the middle ear: the hammer, the anvil, and the stirrup. The vibrations then pass through the oval window, which conducts the vibrations to the cochlea, the inner ear. The cochlea contains the organ of Corti, the hairlike receptor cells of the ear. These cells conduct the perception of sound to the brain.

1. **What are the names of the three bones in the middle ear?**

    _____, _____, and _____

2. **What is the name of the opening that leads to the eardrum?**

    _____

3. **What is the name for the ear's receptor cells?**

    _____

4. **How might your hearing be affected if your eardrum were full of fluid?**

    _____

    _____

 GO ON

SCIENCE

● Lesson 2: Applications (cont.)

Read this passage about regeneration. Use it to answer questions 5–8.

Starfish and crustaceans can regenerate new parts. That means if a starfish's arm or a lobster's claw is cut off, it will grow a new one. People do not generate entire body parts, although there have been instances where young children have grown new fingertips. Starfish and earthworms can regenerate whole new bodies from a part of a body. In the past, this has caused problems for the shellfish industry. Starfish eat oysters, clams, and scallops. This was difficult for the fishermen who hoped to catch these mollusks. The fishermen had been cutting starfish into parts thinking they were killing them. Instead, each part of the starfish would regenerate and create a whole new starfish!

5. **What does it mean to regenerate?**

    _____

    _____

6. **Which of the following would not be able to regenerate a new body part: a starfish, earthworm, lobster, or goldfish?**

    _____

7. **Instead of decreasing the starfish population, what were the fishermen doing by cutting them into pieces?**

    _____

8. **Name one item that is part of the starfish's diet.**

    _____

Now read this short passage on mammals and answer questions 9–11.

A mammal is a vertebrate animal that has hair or fur and feeds milk to its young. How much do you know about mammals?

9. **What mammal can fly?**

    _____

10. **Name a mammal that lives in the ocean.**

    _____

11. **Name a mammal that carries its young in a pouch.**

    _____

SCIENCE
SAMPLE TEST

● **Directions:** Read each question. Fill in the circle for the correct answer.

Examples

A. **Which is not a type of cloud?**

- Ⓐ cirrus
- Ⓑ cumulus
- Ⓒ stratus
- Ⓓ gibbous

B. **Which of these is not a reptile?**

- Ⓕ snake
- Ⓖ turtle
- Ⓗ crocodile
- Ⓙ salamander

For numbers 1–8, read each item. Fill in the circle for your answer or write the answer on the line.

1. **Which type of rock forms from magma?**

   - Ⓐ igneous
   - Ⓑ sedimentary
   - Ⓒ rudimentary
   - Ⓓ metamorphic

2. **Which is the outermost layer of the earth?**

   - Ⓕ core
   - Ⓖ crust
   - Ⓗ mantle
   - Ⓙ rim

3. **How many bones does an adult human have?**

   - Ⓐ 206
   - Ⓑ 300
   - Ⓒ less than 100
   - Ⓓ over 300

4. **Which is not a type of tooth?**

   - Ⓕ incisor
   - Ⓖ feline
   - Ⓗ canine
   - Ⓙ molar

5. **Which is the largest organ of the human body?**

   - Ⓐ the heart
   - Ⓑ the brain
   - Ⓒ the skin
   - Ⓓ the skeleton

6. **What is the seasonal movement of animals from one region to another?**

   - Ⓕ hibernation
   - Ⓖ migration
   - Ⓗ dislocation
   - Ⓙ precipitation

7. **_____ is the bending of light as it passes from one material into another.**

   - Ⓐ Refraction
   - Ⓑ Reflection
   - Ⓒ Luster
   - Ⓓ Filtration

8. **What are the three states of matter?**

   _____

9. **Electric motors transform electrical energy into**

   _____.

   STOP

STUDENT'S NAME

LAST | FIRST | MI

SCHOOL

TEACHER

FEMALE ◯   MALE ◯

BIRTH DATE

MONTH	DAY		YEAR

JAN ◯
FEB ◯
MAR ◯
APR ◯
MAY ◯
JUN ◯
JUL ◯
AUG ◯
SEP ◯
OCT ◯
NOV ◯
DEC ◯

GRADE
⑤ ⑥ ⑦

Part 1: SCIENCE

E1 Ⓐ Ⓑ Ⓒ Ⓓ
E2 Ⓕ Ⓖ Ⓗ Ⓙ
1   Ⓐ Ⓑ Ⓒ Ⓓ
2   Ⓕ Ⓖ Ⓗ Ⓙ
3   Ⓐ Ⓑ Ⓒ Ⓓ
4   Ⓕ Ⓖ Ⓗ Ⓙ
6   Ⓐ Ⓑ Ⓒ Ⓓ
7   Ⓕ Ⓖ Ⓗ Ⓙ

1-57768-976-3 *Spectrum Test Practice 6*

Name _____ Date_____

SCIENCE PRACTICE TEST

● Part 1: Science

Directions: Read each question. Fill in the circle for the correct answer.

Examples

E1. Which is the green substance in plant cells that helps plants make food?	**E2. Which is not part of the nervous system?**
Ⓐ chromosomes	Ⓕ nerve cells
Ⓑ chlorophyll	Ⓖ the spinal cord
Ⓒ photosynthesis	Ⓗ the brain
Ⓓ stomata	Ⓙ the lungs

For numbers 1–8, read each item. Fill in the circle for your answer or write the answer on the line.

1. **Which of these would not be found in a desert ecosystem?**
   Ⓐ cactus
   Ⓑ lizard
   Ⓒ otter
   Ⓓ tortoise

2. **An organism that once lived on the earth but has now died out is _____.**
   Ⓕ endangered
   Ⓖ extinct
   Ⓗ evolved
   Ⓙ energized

3. **Which is not a planet in our solar system?**
   Ⓐ Uranus
   Ⓑ Neptune
   Ⓒ Saturn
   Ⓓ Venice

4. **Which of these is not an invertebrate?**
   Ⓕ squid
   Ⓖ dolphin
   Ⓗ ant
   Ⓙ snail

5. **To discover the age of a tree, you look at its _____.**

6. **Electrical charge builds up when _____.**
   Ⓐ lightning is discharged
   Ⓑ too much current flows through a wire
   Ⓒ positive charges move from one object to another
   Ⓓ negative charges move from one object to another

7. **Which is not a guide to healthy living?**
   Ⓕ stay active every day
   Ⓖ eat a balanced diet
   Ⓗ drink plenty of water
   Ⓙ sleep 4 to 6 hours a night

8. **What is the name of the molten rock beneath the surface of the earth?**
   _____
   _____

SOCIAL STUDIES

● Lesson 1: Concepts

Directions: Read each item. Fill in the circle of the correct answer.

Examples

A. **How many senators from each state serve in the United States Congress?**
- (A) 1
- (B) 2
- (C) 3
- (D) it depends on the population of the state

B. **Which is not a branch of the United States government?**
- (F) legislative
- (G) judicial
- (H) parliament
- (J) executive

 Clue Read each question carefully before choosing an answer. Eliminate answers you know are wrong.

● Practice

1. **Which is not one of the provinces of Canada?**
- (A) Ontario
- (B) Quebec
- (C) Vancouver
- (D) Manitoba

2. **Which is not one of the states of Mexico?**
- (F) San Diego
- (G) Sonora
- (H) Durango
- (J) Veracruz

3. **Which is not a country in Europe?**
- (A) France
- (B) Italy
- (C) Ireland
- (D) Honduras

4. **What is not true of Alexander the Great?**
- (F) He founded the city of Alexandria.
- (G) He built the world's first library in Alexandria.
- (H) During his time, he ruled the entire known world.
- (J) He was an emperor of Ancient Rome.

5. **Which is a strip of land that connects two larger masses of land?**
- (A) peninsula
- (B) isthmus
- (C) islet
- (D) canal

6. **Who was a famous ruler of Ancient Rome?**
- (F) Julius Caesar
- (G) Napoleon Bonaparte
- (H) Attila the Hun
- (J) Charlemagne

7. **From which country did Mexico win independence in 1821?**
- (A) France
- (B) Great Britain
- (C) United States
- (D) Spain

8. **Which is often called the cradle of civilization?**
- (F) France
- (G) Persia
- (H) Mesopotamia
- (J) Greece

 GO ON

Name _____   Date_____

═ SOCIAL STUDIES ═

● Lesson 1: Concepts (cont).

Read each question. Fill in the circle for the correct answer.

9. With what did democracy most likely begin?

    (A) the Revolutionary War

    (B) Babylonian elections

    (C) Greek political ideals

    (D) Egyptian campaigns

10. Which best describes the electoral college in the United States?

    (F) a school where people can gain information about making wise choices when voting

    (G) a system for electing the president and vice president

    (H) a state-to-state connection of equipment that calculates votes

    (J) a university where candidates learn how to conduct a campaign

11. Which statement about elections in the United States is false?

    (A) Some judges are elected, and others are appointed.

    (B) It is possible to have a Democratic president and Republican vice president.

    (C) Voters can cast ballots for local officials, as well as for national officials.

    (D) Members of the House of Representatives and the Senate are elected.

12. Which body of water would not be found on a map of the ancient Middle East?

    (F) Red Sea

    (G) Caspian Sea

    (H) Persian Gulf

    (J) Atlantic Ocean

Use the chart to answer questions 13–15.

13. Which province has the greatest population density?

    _____

14. Which province is the largest in area?

    _____

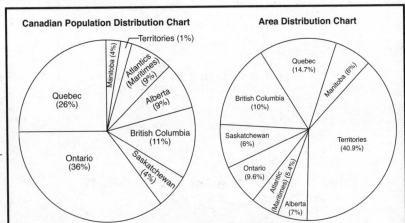

15. Which two provinces together make up more than 60% of the population?

    _____ and _____

STOP

SOCIAL STUDIES

● Lesson 2: Applications

Directions: Look at the map grid below. Use it to answer the questions.

Examples

A. What are the coordinates for San Jose, Costa Rica?

_____

B. What are the coordinates for Havana, Cuba?

_____

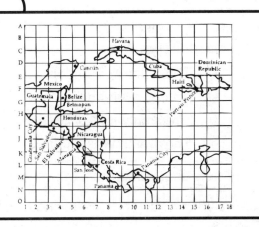

 Read this passage carefully. Then answer the questions.

● Practice

After Julius Caesar's death in 44 B.C., many men vied for control of Rome. The winner was Julius Caesar's great-nephew and adopted son, Octavian. The Senate gave him the title of Augustus, and he became the sole leader of Rome.

Augustus governed Rome from 27 B.C. to A.D. 14. He used his power to stabilize the government of Rome, add many new provinces to the empire, and rebuild the city of Rome after a hundred years of civil war.

The period between 27 B.C. and A.D. 200 is called the Pax Romana, or Roman peace. For almost 200 years, Rome did not participate in any major wars. Instead, the Romans concentrated their efforts on building roads and aqueducts and reconstructing the buildings in the Forum. They also built large amphitheaters, such as the Colosseum, where gladiators fought each other in hand-to-hand

combat. Sometimes the Colosseum was flooded so that mock naval battles could be staged. Romans also enjoyed watching chariot races in the Circus Maximus.

The Roman Empire came to an end soon after A.D. 395 when it was split into the Western Empire and the Eastern Empire. In A.D. 455, barbarians destroyed Rome.

1. How many years did Augustus rule?

_____

2. What was one form of entertainment for the Romans of this time period?

_____

3. Why do you think the Roman Empire was split in two?

_____

_____

_____

Name _____ Date _____

SOCIAL STUDIES
SAMPLE TEST

● **Directions:** Read each question. Fill in the circle for the correct answer.

Examples

A. **What happened at the end of the Peloponnesian Wars?**

Ⓐ The Dark Age ended.

Ⓑ Athens surrendered.

Ⓒ Greek city-states flourished.

Ⓓ The Trojan War began.

B. **Which body of water borders North America on the east?**

Ⓕ Pacific Ocean

Ⓖ Atlantic Ocean

Ⓗ Gulf of Mexico

Ⓙ Mediterranean Sea

For numbers 1–7, read each item. Fill in the circle for your answer or write the answer on the line.

1. **Which of these people did not participate in the Renaissance in Europe?**

Ⓐ Leonardo da Vinci

Ⓑ Michelangelo

Ⓒ Raphael

Ⓓ John Steinbeck

2. **The Aztec civilization was located in the country of _____.**

3. **Which is not a country in South America?**

Ⓕ Chile

Ⓖ Bolivia

Ⓗ Ecuador

Ⓙ Kampuchea

4. **Which of these documents established the first laws of England?**

Ⓐ the Constitution

Ⓑ the Magna Carta

Ⓒ the Declaration of Independence

Ⓓ the Petition of Right

5. **How did the Fertile Crescent get its name?**

Ⓕ It was a fertile island discovered late in the 1900s.

Ⓖ It was an important center of trade.

Ⓗ It sat between two rivers and had rich soil.

Ⓙ It was a mountainous area discovered to be rich in minerals.

6. **Which of these is in the Western Hemisphere?**

Ⓐ Taiwan

Ⓑ Thailand

Ⓒ Tibet

Ⓓ Peru

7. **Describe the meaning of the term "supply and demand."**

_____

_____

ANSWER SHEET

STUDENT'S NAME																	
LAST											FIRST						MI
A	A	A	A	A	A	A	A	A	A	A	A	A	A	A	A	A	A
B	B	B	B	B	B	B	B	B	B	B	B	B	B	B	B	B	B
C	C	C	C	C	C	C	C	C	C	C	C	C	C	C	C	C	C
D	D	D	D	D	D	D	D	D	D	D	D	D	D	D	D	D	D
E	E	E	E	E	E	E	E	E	E	E	E	E	E	E	E	E	E
F	F	F	F	F	F	F	F	F	F	F	F	F	F	F	F	F	F
G	G	G	G	G	G	G	G	G	G	G	G	G	G	G	G	G	G
H	H	H	H	H	H	H	H	H	H	H	H	H	H	H	H	H	H
I	I	I	I	I	I	I	I	I	I	I	I	I	I	I	I	I	I
J	J	J	J	J	J	J	J	J	J	J	J	J	J	J	J	J	J
K	K	K	K	K	K	K	K	K	K	K	K	K	K	K	K	K	K
L	L	L	L	L	L	L	L	L	L	L	L	L	L	L	L	L	L
M	M	M	M	M	M	M	M	M	M	M	M	M	M	M	M	M	M
N	N	N	N	N	N	N	N	N	N	N	N	N	N	N	N	N	N
O	O	O	O	O	O	O	O	O	O	O	O	O	O	O	O	O	O
P	P	P	P	P	P	P	P	P	P	P	P	P	P	P	P	P	P
Q	Q	Q	Q	Q	Q	Q	Q	Q	Q	Q	Q	Q	Q	Q	Q	Q	Q
R	R	R	R	R	R	R	R	R	R	R	R	R	R	R	R	R	R
S	S	S	S	S	S	S	S	S	S	S	S	S	S	S	S	S	S
T	T	T	T	T	T	T	T	T	T	T	T	T	T	T	T	T	T
U	U	U	U	U	U	U	U	U	U	U	U	U	U	U	U	U	U
V	V	V	V	V	V	V	V	V	V	V	V	V	V	V	V	V	V
W	W	W	W	W	W	W	W	W	W	W	W	W	W	W	W	W	W
X	X	X	X	X	X	X	X	X	X	X	X	X	X	X	X	X	X
Y	Y	Y	Y	Y	Y	Y	Y	Y	Y	Y	Y	Y	Y	Y	Y	Y	Y
Z	Z	Z	Z	Z	Z	Z	Z	Z	Z	Z	Z	Z	Z	Z	Z	Z	Z

SCHOOL

TEACHER

FEMALE ◯ MALE ◯

BIRTH DATE				
MONTH	DAY		YEAR	
JAN ◯	0	0		0
FEB ◯	1	1		1
MAR ◯	2	2		2
APR ◯	3	3		3
MAY ◯		4		4
JUN ◯		5	5	5
JUL ◯		6	6	6
AUG ◯		7	7	7
SEP ◯		8	8	8
OCT ◯		9	9	9
NOV ◯			0	
DEC ◯				

GRADE

5 6 7

Part 1: SOCIAL STUDIES

E1	A B C D
E2	F G H J
1	A B C D
2	F G H J
3	A B C D
5	F G H J
6	A B C D

SOCIAL STUDIES PRACTICE TEST

● Part 1: Social Studies

Directions: Read each item. Write an answer or fill in the circle for the correct answer.

Examples

E1. Which of these is a province of Canada?

- Ⓐ Nova Scotia
- Ⓑ New Zealand
- Ⓒ New England
- Ⓓ Tierra del Fuego

E2. In which country will you find the Rhine?

- Ⓕ Norway
- Ⓖ Great Britain
- Ⓗ Germany
- Ⓙ Spain

---

1. **Which of these is a product cycle?**
   - Ⓐ A person buys a new car and then takes it to the car wash.
   - Ⓑ A company sells car parts to an automobile manufacturer, who creates a car and sells it to a dealer; the dealer sells it to a consumer.
   - Ⓒ A company that sells car parts declares bankruptcy and then reorganizes its corporation under a new name.
   - Ⓓ A company manufactures cars, creates advertising to promote the cars, and then raises prices on its cars to make more money.

2. **Which of these countries is not a member of the European Union?**
   - Ⓕ France
   - Ⓖ Belgium
   - Ⓗ Norway
   - Ⓙ Spain

3. **Which of these was not an aspect of Incan culture?**
   - Ⓐ roads
   - Ⓑ bridges
   - Ⓒ a royal family
   - Ⓓ a written language

4. **Describe how the Incan culture came to an end. Who conquered the Incas?**

   _____

   _____

   _____

5. **Which of these is a famous Incan ruin?**
   - Ⓕ Lima
   - Ⓖ Huangayo
   - Ⓗ Machu Picchu
   - Ⓙ Pisco

6. **What was the name used for the lowest class of workers who were ruled by knights and lords in medieval culture?**
   - Ⓐ peasants
   - Ⓑ farmers
   - Ⓒ serfs
   - Ⓓ pages

7. **What is cuneiform?**

   _____

   _____

STOP

ANSWER KEY

READING: VOCABULARY
Lesson 1: Synonyms
• Page 11
- A. B
- B. G
- 1. C
- 2. G
- 3. C
- 4. H
- 5. A
- 6. J
- 7. C
- 8. G

READING: VOCABULARY
Lesson 2: Vocabulary Skills
• Page 12
- A. A
- B. G
- 1. A
- 2. H
- 3. D
- 4. H
- 5. A
- 6. F
- 7. B
- 8. J

READING: VOCABULARY
Lesson 3: Antonyms
• Page 13
- A. C
- B. F
- 1. A
- 2. F
- 3. B
- 4. G
- 5. D
- 6. G
- 7. D
- 8. G

READING: VOCABULARY
Lesson 4: Multi-Meaning Words
• Page 14
- A. B
- B. G
- 1. C
- 2. G
- 3. C
- 4. G

READING: VOCABULARY
Lesson 5: Words in Context
• Page 15
- A. D
- B. F
- 1. B
- 2. F
- 3. C
- 4. J
- 5. C
- 6. H

READING: VOCABULARY
Lesson 6: Word Study
• Page 16
- A. B
- B. G
- 1. B
- 2. G
- 3. C
- 4. J

- 5. C
- 6. F

READING: VOCABULARY SAMPLE TEST
• Pages 17–20
- E1. C
- E2. G
- 1. C
- 2. F
- 3. B
- 4. H
- 5. A
- 6. H
- 7. B
- 8. H
- 9. A
- 10. G
- 11. A
- 12. G
- 13. A
- 14. H
- 15. C
- 16. J
- 17. D
- 18. G
- 19. C
- 20. H
- 21. B
- 22. H
- 23. D
- 24. H
- 25. B
- 26. F
- 27. B
- 28. G
- 29. C
- 30. H
- 31. A
- 32. J
- 33. B
- 34. F
- 35. C

READING: READING COMPREHENSION
Lesson 7: Main Idea
• Page 21
- A. A
- 1. D
- 2. G

READING: READING COMPREHENSION
Lesson 8: Recalling Details
• Page 22
- A. C
- 1. B
- 2. H

READING: READING COMPREHENSION
Lesson 9: Drawing Conclusions
• Pages 23–24
- A. A
- 1. B
- 2. H
- B. F
- 3. B
- 4. G

READING: READING COMPREHENSION
Lesson 10: Fact and Opinion & Cause and Effect
• Page 25
- A. C
- 1. D
- 2. G

READING: READING COMPREHENSION
Lesson 11: Story Elements
• Page 26
- A. C
- 1. C
- 2. G

READING: READING COMPREHENSION
Lesson 12: Fiction
• Page 27
- A. B
- 1. A
- 2. G

READING: READING COMPREHENSION
Lesson 13: Fiction
• Pages 28–29
- A. B
- 1. B
- 2. H
- 3. B
- 4. H
- 5. B
- 6. F

READING: READING COMPREHENSION
Lesson 14: Fiction
• Pages 30–31
- A. C
- 1. C
- 2. J
- 3. C
- 4. G
- 5. A
- 6. G

READING: READING COMPREHENSION
Lesson 15: Nonfiction
• Page 32
- A. B
- 1. B
- 2. J

READING: READING COMPREHENSION
Lesson 16: Nonfiction
• Pages 33–34
- A. D
- 1. A
- 2. J
- 3. D
- 4. H
- 5. B
- 6. G

Published by Spectrum. Copyright protected.
1-57768-976-3 Spectrum Test Practice 6

ANSWER KEY

READING: READING COMPREHENSION
Lesson 17: Nonfiction
• Pages 35–36
- A. B
- 1. B
- 2. G
- 3. A
- 4. G
- 5. C

READING: READING COMPREHENSION SAMPLE TEST
• Pages 37–40
- E1. C
- 1. B
- 2. H
- 3. A
- 4. J
- 5. B
- 6. F
- E2. F
- 7. A
- 8. H
- 9. B
- 10. F
- 11. A

READING PRACTICE TEST
Part 1: Vocabulary
• Pages 42–45
- E1. A
- E2. G
- 1. C
- 2. H
- 3. A
- 4. G
- 5. C
- 6. F
- 7. C
- 8. F
- 9. C
- 10. G
- 11. A
- 12. G
- 13. C
- 14. G
- 15. B
- 16. H
- 17. B
- 18. H
- 19. B
- 20. G
- 21. C
- 22. F
- 23. D
- 24. H
- 25. C
- 26. G
- 27. A
- 28. H
- 29. B
- 30. H
- 31. A
- 32. G
- 33. C
- 34. J
- 35. B

READING PRACTICE TEST
Part 2: Reading Comprehension
• Pages 46–55
- E1. B
- 1. D
- 2. J
- 3. B
- 4. J
- 5. A
- 6. J
- 7. B
- 8. J
- 9. C
- 10. J
- 11. A
- 12. G
- 13. D
- 14. H
- 15. A
- 16. G
- 17. B
- 18. H
- 19. B
- 20. J
- 21. A
- 22. H
- 23. B
- 24. G
- 25. B
- 26. F
- 27. B
- 28. F
- 29. D

LANGUAGE: LANGUAGE MECHANICS
Lesson 1: Punctuation
• Pages 56–57
- A. B
- B. J
- 1. B
- 2. J
- 3. C
- 4. G
- 5. C
- 6. H
- 7. A
- 8. G
- 9. A
- 10. H
- 11. A
- 12. F
- 13. C
- 14. G
- 15. A
- 16. H

LANGUAGE: LANGUAGE MECHANICS
Lesson 2: Capitalization and Punctuation
• Pages 58–60
- A. B
- B. J
- 1. D
- 2. H
- 3. C
- 4. H
- 5. B
- 6. J

- 7. B
- 8. H
- 9. D
- 10. F
- 11. B
- 12. H
- 13. C
- 14. G
- 15. A
- 16. J
- 17. B
- 18. H
- 19. A
- 20. G

LANGUAGE: LANGUAGE MECHANICS SAMPLE TEST
• Pages 61–64
- E1. B
- 1. A
- 2. G
- 3. D
- 4. G
- 5. A
- 6. F
- 7. B
- 8. G
- 9. A
- 10. F
- 11. B
- 12. F
- 13. C
- 14. H
- 15. B
- 16. H
- 17. A
- 18. H
- 19. A
- 20. J
- 21. C
- 22. J
- 23. B
- 24. H
- 25. A
- 26. J
- 27. C
- 28. G
- 29. C

LANGUAGE: LANGUAGE EXPRESSION
Lesson 3: Usage
• Pages 65–67
- A. B
- B. J
- 1. B
- 2. H
- 3. A
- 4. H
- 5. D
- 6. F
- 7. B
- 8. H
- 9. D
- 10. F
- 11. B
- 12. F
- 13. B
- 14. J
- 15. D

16. G
17. A
18. H
19. D

LANGUAGE: LANGUAGE EXPRESSION
Lesson 4: Sentences
• Pages 68–70

A. B
B. H
C. C
1. B
2. G
3. B
4. G
5. B
6. G
7. D
8. G
9. D
10. H
11. B
12. G
13. C
14. H
15. C

LANGUAGE: LANGUAGE EXPRESSION
Lesson 5: Paragraphs
• Pages 71–74

A. B
1. C
2. G
3. A
4. H
5. C
6. G
7. A
8. H
9. D
10. H
11. B
12. F
13. B
14. H

LANGUAGE: LANGUAGE EXPRESSION SAMPLE TEST
• Pages 75–78

E1. C
1. C
2. F
3. B
4. F
5. A
6. G
7. C
8. G
9. A
10. F
11. C
12. H
13. B
14. J
15. B
16. H
17. B
18. B
19. C

20. F

LANGUAGE: SPELLING
Lesson 6: Spelling Skills
• Pages 79–80

A. C
B. G
1. B
2. F
3. C
4. G
5. C
6. F
7. C
8. F
9. D
10. H
11. B
12. F
13. B
14. H
15. A
16. J
17. C
18. G

LANGUAGE: SPELLING SAMPLE TEST
• Pages 81–82

E1. B
E2. H
1. B
2. H
3. D
4. G
5. C
6. G
7. B
8. H
9. A
10. G
11. C
12. F
13. D
14. G
15. A
16. H
17. B
18. J
19. A
20. J

LANGUAGE: STUDY SKILLS
Lesson 7: Study Skills
• Pages 83–84

A. D
1. A
2. G
3. D
4. H
5. C
6. G
7. B
8. J
9. B
10. G
11. C
12. J
13. D

LANGUAGE: STUDY SKILLS SAMPLE TEST
• Pages 85–87

E1. C
E2. J
1. A
2. J
3. B
4. F
5. C
6. G
7. C
8. G
9. C
10. G
11. C
12. F
13. C
14. G
15. B
16. J
17. C
18. G

LANGUAGE PRACTICE TEST
Part 1: Language Mechanics
• Pages 89–99

E1. B
1. C
2. H
3. D
4. G
5. A
6. J
7. B
8. H
9. B
10. J
11. C
12. J
13. C
14. F
15. D
16. J
17. B
18. H
19. D
20. F
21. B

Part 2: Language Expression

E1. C
1. C
2. J
3. B
4. F
5. D
6. G
7. C
8. H
9. D
10. G
11. D
12. G
13. C
14. H
15. C
16. G
17. D
18. G

19. A
20. G

Part 3: Spelling
E1. B
E2. H
1. A
2. F
3. B
4. F
5. C
6. H
7. A
8. G
9. D
10. F
11. B
12. H
13. A
14. F
15. B
16. H
17. D
18. F
19. A
20. G

Part 4: Study Skills
E1. B
1. D
2. G
3. C
4. G
5. B
6. F
7. D
8. H
9. C
10. F

MATH: CONCEPTS
Lesson 1: Numeration
• Pages 100–101
A. D
B. H
1. B
2. H
3. A
4. G
5. C
6. G
7. A
8. H
9. D
10. H
11. D
12. H
13. A
14. H
15. C
16. F

MATH: CONCEPTS
Lesson 2: Numeration
• Pages 102–103
A. B
B. G
1. C
2. G
3. D
4. F
5. C

6. H
7. D
8. G
9. B
10. G
11. A
12. J
13. C
14. J
15. D

MATH: CONCEPTS
Lesson 3: Properties
• Pages 104–105
A. A
B. H
1. B
2. H
3. C
4. G
5. B
6. H
7. B
8. H
9. B
10. G
11. B

MATH: CONCEPTS
Lesson 4: Fractions and Decimals
• Pages 106–107
A. D
1. B
2. H
3. C
4. F
5. A
6. G
7. B
8. F
9. C
10. F
11. D
12. G
13. B

MATH: CONCEPTS
SAMPLE TEST
• Pages 108–109
E1. C
E2. F
1. C
2. G
3. A
4. H
5. D
6. G
7. C
8. F
9. B
10. H
11. A
12. H
13. C
14. G
15. C

MATH: COMPUTATION
Lesson 5: Whole Numbers (All Operations)
• Page 110
A. C

B. J
1. C
2. F
3. B
4. J
5. A
6. G
7. C
8. J

MATH: COMPUTATION
Lesson 6: Addition and Subtraction of Fractions
• Page 111
A. D
B. G
1. B
2. F
3. B
4. H
5. C
6. J
7. D
8. G

MATH: COMPUTATION
Lesson 7: Multiplication of Fractions
• Page 112
A. B
B. F
1. B
2. G
3. D
4. J
5. A
6. G
7. C
8. J

MATH: COMPUTATION
Lesson 8: Division of Fractions
• Page 113
A. B
B. G
1. C
2. F
3. D
4. F
5. B
6. F
7. C
8. G

MATH: COMPUTATION
Lesson 9: Addition and Subtraction of Decimals
• Page 114
A. C
B. H
1. D
2. H
3. D
4. H
5. D
6. F
7. B
8. G

MATH: COMPUTATION
Lesson 10: Multiplication of Decimals
• Page 115
A. B
B. G
1. C
2. H
3. B
4. J
5. A
6. G
7. A
8. H

MATH: COMPUTATION
Lesson 11: Division of Decimals
• Page 116
A. C
B. J
1. B
2. G
3. C
4. F
5. C
6. J
7. A
8. G

MATH: COMPUTATION SAMPLE TEST
• Pages 117–118
E1. B
E2. H
1. B
2. F
3. B
4. G
5. C
6. F
7. D
8. G
9. D
10. H
11. B
12. F
13. B
14. H
15. B
16. G
17. B
18. H
19. B
20. J
21. D
22. G

MATH: APPLICATIONS
Lesson 12: Geometry
• Pages 119–121
A. B
1. B
2. G
3. B
4. F
5. A
6. H
7. B
8. H
9. A
10. G

11. B
12. H
13. A
14. H
15. C
16. J
17. D

MATH: APPLICATIONS
Lesson 13: Measurement
• Page 122
A. B
1. A
2. G
3. B
4. G
5. C
6. G
7. A
8. J
9. A
10. H
11. B
12. G

MATH: APPLICATIONS
Lesson 14: Problem Solving
• Pages 124–127
A. B
B. G
1. B
2. G
3. A
4. J
5. C
6. H
7. A
8. F
9. B
10. F
11. B
12. F
13. A
14. G
15. A
16. F
17. A
18. G
19. C
20. G
21. B
22. G
23. A
24. G

MATH: APPLICATIONS
Lesson 15: Algebra
• Page 128
A. B
B. F
1. B
2. G
3. B
4. J
5. A

MATH: APPLICATIONS SAMPLE TEST
• Pages 129–132
E1. B
E2. G
1. B

2. H
3. B
4. F
5. B
6. G
7. B
8. G
9. C
10. J
11. B
12. F
13. B
14. F
15. C
16. J
17. B
18. G
19. A
20. G
21. B
22. H
23. A
24. H

MATH PRACTICE TEST
Part 1: Concepts
• Pages 134–136
E1. D
E2. H
1. A
2. G
3. B
4. F
5. C
6. H
7. D
8. H
9. C
10. J
11. C
12. H
13. B
14. G
15. D
16. J
17. A
18. G
19. B
20. G
21. D
22. H
23. A
24. J
25. A

MATH PRACTICE TEST
Part 2: Computation
• Pages 137–138
E1. B
E2. G
1. A
2. G
3. B
4. H
5. C
6. F
7. D
8. G
9. C
10. G

ANSWER KEY

11. C
12. H
13. B
14. H
15. D
16. F
17. C
18. H
19. A
20. H
21. B
22. F

MATH PRACTICE TEST
Part 3: Applications
• Pages 139–141

E1. B
E2. G
1. A
2. G
3. A
4. G
5. A
6. J
7. B
8. H
9. A
10. G
11. A
12. G
13. B
14. G
15. B
16. H
17. C
18. G

SCIENCE
Lesson 1: Concepts
• Pages 142–143

A. C
B. J
1. B
2. F
3. B
4. H
5. B
6. H
7. A
8. G
9. C
10. J
11. B
12. F
13. B
14. J
15. B

SCIENCE
Lesson 2: Applications
• Pages 144–145

E1. A. Answers will vary.
    B. Answers will vary.
1. hammer, anvil, and stirrup
2. auditory canal
3. organ of Corti
4. You would probably have trouble hearing out of that ear.
5. to grow a new part
6. goldfish
7. They were increasing the starfish population.
8. oysters, clams, or scallops
9. bat
10. whale, dolphin, others
11. any marsupial

SCIENCE SAMPLE TEST
• Page 146

A. D
B. J
1. A
2. G
3. A
4. G
5. C
6. G
7. A
8. solid, liquid, and gas
9. mechanical energy

SCIENCE PRACTICE TEST
• Page 148

E1. B
E2. J
1. C
2. G
3. D
4. G
5. rings
6. D
7. J
8. lava

SOCIAL STUDIES
Lesson 1: Concepts
• Pages 149–150

A. B
B. H
1. C
2. F
3. D
4. J
5. B
6. F
7. D
8. J
9. C
10. G
11. B
12. J
13. Ontario
14. Quebec
15. Quebec and Ontario

SOCIAL STUDIES
Lesson 2: Applications
• Page 151

A. L-7
B. C-9
1. 41 years
2. chariot races, watching gladiators, or watching mock naval battles
3. It became too large to rule. Other answers are possible.

SOCIAL STUDIES SAMPLE TEST
• Page 152

A. B
B. G
1. D
2. Mexico
3. J
4. B
5. H
6. D
7. Answers will vary. Supply and demand are the forces that determine the amount of product produced and its price. In basic terms, the supply of a product is determined by the user's demand for a product.

SOCIAL STUDIES PRACTICE TEST
• Page 154

E1. A
E2. H
1. B
2. H
3. D
4. The Spanish captured and executed the Incan emperor. Without a leader, the Spanish easily took over the empire.
5. H
6. C
7. an ancient writing system